DARKWATER

CLASSICS IN BLACK STUDIES

DARKWATER

W. E. B. Du Bois

WITH AN INTRODUCTION BY

Joe R. Feagin

Humanity
Books

an imprint of Prometheus Books
59 John Glenn Drive, Amherst, New York 14228-2197

Cover image reproduced from the *Dictionary of American Portraits*,
Dover Publications, Inc., 1967

Published by Humanity Books, an imprint of Prometheus Books

Introduction copyright © 2003 by Joe R. Feagin.

Inquiries should be addressed to
Humanity Books
59 John Glenn Drive
Amherst, New York 14228–2197
VOICE: 716–691–0133, ext. 207
FAX: 716–564–2711
WWW.PROMETHEUSBOOKS.COM

07 06 05 04 03   5 4 3 2 1

Library of Congress Cataloging-in-Publication Data

Du Bois, W. E. B. (William Edward Burghardt), 1868–1963.
    Darkwater : voices from within the veil / W.E.B. Du Bois ; with an introduction by Joe R. Feagin.
        p. cm. — (Classics in Black studies series)
    Originally published: New York : Harcourt, Brace, and Howe, 1920. With new introd.
    ISBN 1–59102–057–3 (pbk. : alk. paper)
    1. United States—Race relations. 2. African Americans. I. Title.
II. Classics in Black studies.

E185.61 .D83 2002
305.896'073—dc21   2002038944

Printed in the United States of America on acid-free paper

W. E. B. (William Edward Burghardt) Du Bois was born on February 23, 1868, in Great Barrington, Massachusetts. Du Bois's father, Alfred, left home soon after Du Bois was born, and he was raised by his mother, Mary Burghardt Du Bois, a household domestic. The Burghardt family had been well established in the community for generations, with members working as housemaids, waiters, and small farmers. One of his great-grandfathers had fought in the American Revolution.

After graduating as valedictorian from high school in 1884, Du Bois attended Fisk University in Nashville, Tennessee, receiving his bachelor of arts in 1888. That same year he entered Harvard University and earned a bachelor of arts cum laude in philosophy in 1890. He received his master of arts in history from Harvard in 1891, and from 1892 to 1894 engaged in graduate study in history and economics at the University of Berlin on a Slater Fund fellowship. In 1895 he earned his doctorate in history from Harvard. His dissertation, *The Suppression of the African Slave Trade to the United States of America, 1638–1870*, was pub-

lished in 1896 as Number 1 in the Harvard Historical
Studies series. From 1894 to 1896 he taught Latin and
Greek at Wilberforce University in Ohio.

Du Bois became an assistant in sociology from 1896 to
1897 at the University of Pennsylvania. He studied
Philadelphia's slums and his pioneering sociological study
The Philadelphia Negro: A Social Study was published in 1899.

From 1897 to 1910 Du Bois was professor of economics
and history at Atlanta University, and from 1897 to 1914 he
edited its annual studies of Black life.

Du Bois clashed with educator Booker T. Washington
over Washington's acceptance of racial discrimination. In
1905 Du Bois became a founder and general secretary of
the Niagara movement, which called for full civil, political,
and social rights for Black Americans. The Niagara movement declined and in 1909 he was one of the founders of
the National Association for the Advancement of Colored
People (NAACP). From 1910 to 1934 he served on the
NAACP's board of directors, and was its director of pub-
licity and research, editing its monthly magazine, the *Crisis*.

In 1934 Du Bois resigned from the NAACP in a debate
over the goals of one-way integration versus Black community development. Du Bois advocated African
American–controlled schools, institutions, and businesses.
He returned to Atlanta University, serving as chair of the
department of sociology from 1934 to 1944. In 1940 he
founded the social science quarterly *Phylon*.

Politically, Du Bois was a member of the Socialist Party
from 1910 to 1912. He attended peace congresses in New
York, Paris, and Moscow in 1949. In 1950 he was asked by
the American Labor Party of New York to run for the U.S.
Senate. He was defeated in the November 1950 election,
but he garnered 4 percent of the electorate.

Long active in the peace movement, Du Bois served as chair of the Peace Information Center, which circulated the "Stockholm Appeal," calling for the ban of atomic weapons. The U.S. Department of Justice demanded that the center register "as an agent of a foreign principal." Although the center had no ties to the Soviet Union, and was dissolved on October 12, 1950, Du Bois and five others were indicted as agents of a foreign power. The government's case collapsed and the defendants were acquitted.

Convinced that the American Communist Party would provide the United States with a viable third party, Du Bois joined this organization in 1961. That same year he took up residence in Ghana, Africa, becoming a citizen of that country in 1963.

A prolific writer, Du Bois published over one hundred articles and essays, and authored twenty-one books, including two novels: *The Quest of the Silver Fleece* (1911) and *Dark Princess: A Romance* (1928); a book of essays and poetry: *Darkwater: Voices from within the Veil* (1920); and histories of Black people: *The Negro* (1915), *The Gift of Black Folk: Negroes in the Making of America* (1924), *Black Reconstruction in America, 1860–1880* (1935), and *Black Folk, Then and Now* (1939). He was a fellow and life member of the American Association for the Advancement of Science and a member of the National Institute of Arts and Letters.

W. E. B. Du Bois died in Ghana on August 27, 1963.

INTRODUCTION

In *Darkwater: Voices from within the Veil*, the distinguished American scholar W. E. B. Du Bois presents a set of provocative essays on racial matters unrivaled in perceptiveness for their time. Indeed, the insights in some essays remain unrivaled in our time. This collection was first published in 1920 by the new company of Harcourt, Brace & Howe. Like his classic book *The Souls of Black Folk*, Du Bois's masterpiece *Darkwater* is not only original and probing in its brilliant ideas but also experimental in its presentation, ranging from detailed sociopolitical analyses to lyrical and poetic presentations.

The book has ten major chapters, beginning with an autobiographical piece and ending with a chilling science-fiction story about the destruction of New York City. In between, there are eight articles of sociological, economic, and political analysis, with brief fiction and poetry bridges mixed in, mainly at the ends of chapters. Some chapters and poetic interludes had been previously published, in such places as the NAACP's magazine the *Crisis* and in the *Atlantic Monthly*. In the book's postscript Du Bois accents the signif-

icance of his positioning poetic "tributes to beauty" among
his "sterner flights of logic." The two presentation method-
ologies complement and extend one another, and thereby
offer a lesson for contemporary authors.

In an opening *Credo*, Du Bois articulates what would
now be called the philosophy of multiculturalism: "I believe
that all men, black and brown and white, are brothers,
varying through time and opportunity, in form and gift and
feature, but differing in no essential particular, and alike in
soul and the possibility of infinite development" (p. 33).
Then he adds a statement that some have seen as racial
chauvinism: "Especially do I believe in the Negro Race: in
the beauty of its genius, the sweetness of its soul, and its
strength in that meekness which shall yet inherit this turbulent earth" (p. 33). This comment can be construed as
racially chauvinistic only if the reader is insensitive to the
impact of racism and takes the statement out of the multicultural, multiracial context in which Du Bois offers it. For
him, it is the *human race* that is central, and the darker peoples of the world may yet be the salvation of that human
race. Indeed, a key argument throughout *Darkwater*, as the
subtitle "Voices from within the Veil" indicates, is that those
behind the veil of racial subordination can see much better
into what Whites and White society are about, than Whites
can see into the realities of racially subordinated groups.

In chapter 1, "The Shadow of Years," Du Bois revisits
some biographical details of his life, details that he presented
in various ways in a number of his books. Born of free
African Americans in western Massachusetts, Du Bois
writes eloquently of his ancestors. Noting that the Du Bois
side of his family had a strong mixed-race heritage, he
describes how he grew up among small farmers, with a

---

*Pagination in this edition.

mother who was patient and determined and a father who, he says, was a dreamer, unreliable, and a poet. Slowly, he became painfully aware that some local Whites viewed his "brown skin a misfortune; once or twice I became painfully aware that some human beings even thought it a crime" (p. 40). Nonetheless, the racist actions that he regularly encountered did not slow him down in his life's efforts, including his school studies, although he did shed some "secret tears" over his racial persecution. After he graduated from high school with high honors, a distinctive achievement for a young African American facing overt racism, he dreamed of attending Harvard. Because of difficult economic circumstances, however, he went to a historically Black institution, Fisk University, in Nashville, Tennessee. In his senior year at Fisk, he was accepted at Harvard and entered as a junior. Graduating from Harvard in 1888, he began graduate work in U.S. history. Later, he would graduate with the first Ph.D. degree given by Harvard to an African American.

In this autobiographical chapter Du Bois recounts briefly his first experience doing empirical research in the new field of sociology, in which he was an early pioneer. Laboring "morning, noon, and night," he conducted the first empirical study of urban Black Americans, a mid-1890s field study published as *The Philadelphia Negro*. In this study he combined survey research methods and a descriptive statistical analysis with some qualitative data and historical analysis of the community studied.

Chapter 2 of *Darkwater*, titled "The Souls of White Folk," is the first major analysis in Western intellectual history to probe deeply White identity and the meaning of Whiteness. In this original and provocative analysis, Du Bois argues effectively that "the discovery of personal whiteness among the world's people is a very modern thing. . . . The ancient world would have laughed at such a distinction. . . . Today, we have changed all that, and the world in a sudden, emotional conversion has discovered that it is white and by that token, wonderful!" (p. 56). In a trenchant assessment he explores the arrogance of the White perspective that claims "title to the universe" and that, by emphasis or omission, tries to "make children believe that every great soul the world ever saw was a white man's soul" (p. 57). Furthermore, Whites have brought a great "descent to Hell" for the globe's peoples of color. White actions are buttressed by a "deep and passionate hatred" of peoples of color. Rhetorically, Du Bois asks Whites what they would say "if the next census were to report that half of black America was dead and the other half dying" (p. 59). He implies that many would be happy to be rid of African Americans. He later chides Whites for failing to live up to their own moralistic rhetoric; indeed, "the number of white individuals who are practising with even reasonable approximation the democracy and unselfishness of Jesus Christ is so small and unimportant as to be fit subject for jest in Sunday supplements . . ." (p. 61).

One of the most important dimensions of this challenging book is its recurring global sensitivity and perspective. Chapter 2 and the other essays often go beyond U.S. racism to its global context. For example, Du Bois notes that, while the U.S. government protests against brutality on the part of European governments, it ignores racial atrocities at home. Du Bois also makes important connections between the unjust enrichment of White Europeans over recent centuries and the unjust impoverishment of people of African ancestry. The greatness of Europe, which Du Bois fully acknowledges, comes from the strength of its foundation, a foundation built upon the ideas, sciences, economic developments, and mineral resources of many parts of the globe, but especially those of Africa and Asia. Du Bois worked from a conceptual perspective critically assessing the global racial order, perhaps the first social theorist to do so. Writing about the years around 1900, he contends that, "White supremacy was all but world-wide, Africa was dead, India conquered, Japan isolated, and China prostrate, while white America whetted her sword for mongrel Mexico and mulatto South America. . . . The using of men for the benefit of masters is no new invention of modern Europe. . . . But Europe proposed to apply it on a scale and with an elaborateness of detail of which no former world ever dreamed. The imperial width of the thing,—the heaven-defying audacity—makes its modern newness" (pp. 66–67). The brutal exploitation of African labor and land had long been omitted from most historical accounts of European affluence, as it often is today.

In other writings Du Bois documented the point that the enslavement of Africans in the Americas was more extreme than slavery in ancient societies such as the Roman Empire. An essential feature of North American slavery was the denial of almost all human liberties. Slaves "could own nothing; they could make no contracts; they could hold no property; nor traffic in property; they could not hire out; they could not legally marry . . . they could not appeal from their master; they could be punished at will."[1]

Chapter 3, "The Hands of Ethiopia," further expands Du Bois's global perspective. Much of this chapter appeared in a 1915 article for the *Atlantic Monthly* under the title, "The African Roots of the War." Here Du Bois further develops his argument that modern capitalism has generated much wealth off the backs of African peoples. For four centuries Europe was the "chief support of that trade in human beings which first and last robbed black Africa of a hundred million human beings" (p. 80). In addition to building the Atlantic slave trade, Europeans went to Africa to build their industry "on a new slavery" depriving Africans of their land and mineral resources. Moreover, he suggests that White elites discovered that the White working classes, who were starting to rebel against class domination in Europe and America, could be held in check by convincing the latter that they were racially superior to workers of color across the globe. Here Du Bois anticipates the idea of the "psychological wage of whiteness," a view that would develop later in his historical book *Black Reconstruction*. He pursues this idea again in chapter 4 here.

In chapter 3 Du Bois, who is often considered the "father of Pan-Africanism," offers one of the first postcolonial analyses, and with it some postcolonial visions. He is very concerned with freeing Africa from European colonialism and with restoring control over African resources to Africans. He was a major organizer of, and key participant in, the four Pan-African conferences in 1919–1927, and again in the fifth conference at the end of World War II. Held in Manchester, England, that powerful 1945 conference hosted many of the leaders who were then working for, and in, a postcolonial Africa. There they celebrated the distinguished Du Bois for his anticolonial writings and activism.

Du Bois begins chapter 4, "Of Work and Wealth," with reflections on teaching history, economy, and sociology while he was at Atlanta University. He articulates well the dilemma of the Black teacher who is often asked by his students, "Do you trust White people?" As Du Bois poignantly recounts it, the Black teacher usually feels that he must dissimulate in reply: "Yet you rise and lie and say you do; you must say it for her salvation and the world's; you repeat that she must trust

them, that most white folks are honest, and all the while you
are lying and every level, silent eye there knows you are
lying . . ." (p. 102). The chapter proceeds to deal with how
White workers have driven Black workers out of the new
industrial unions, to the detriment of both groups. He notes
the recent anti-Black rioting by Whites in East St. Louis,
where many Blacks were killed and injured by White workers
fearful of losing jobs to Black workers. Here Du Bois
develops the beginnings of a critique of modern capitalism,
a critique that shows how a small capitalist elite gains wealth
at the expense of the working class—with the Whites in that
working class coming to view Black workers as competitors
rather than allies. Why do they do this? Because White
workers have come to support the society's racial hierarchy,
with its privileges, opportunities, and resources for Whites.
They have adopted as well the rationalizing ideology of
White superiority. Again, Du Bois notes that White workers
have accepted the psychological wage of Whiteness. He then
adds yet another astute insight that "the freeing of the black
slaves freed America," by which he means that full U.S. social
and economic development would not have been possible
without the abolition of slavery (p. 117). He carries this
insight further and argues that White elites' abandonment of
ownership of human beings must of necessity be followed by
abandonment of elite ownership of the means of capitalistic
production (such as factories), which are produced by
workers working collectively.

Chapter 5, " 'The Servant in the House,' " deals forcefully with the ways in which many African Americans,
including Du Bois's mother and Du Bois himself, have
labored for centuries in various forms of menial service for
Whites, for very low wages and suffering recurring insults
to human dignity. This servile condition Du Bois views as

an anachronism and "medieval barbarism" that survives into
the modern period. No one wants to be a servant, he suggests, but many want to have servants. Why does this oppressive phenomenon of low-wage, menial service persist?
Du Bois suggests, in an aphoristic phrase, that U.S. society
still holds, consciously or unconsciously, to a "manure
theory of civilization." This is the view that there is a sub-
terranean area of work which no civilized person should
want to do, but which must be done for the larger society
by "derelicts" and "half-men," such as oppressed African
Americans who have been degraded into such servile positions by White Americans. U.S. "democracy," he adds with
acerbity, is built upon the foundation of menial labor.

In chapter 6, "Of the Ruling of Men," Du Bois develops
additional ideas in political sociology, particularly ideas on
how the "ruling of men" develops in societies. Over the
course of history, he notes, we have seen the expansion of
human knowledge and political suffrage, with growing numbers of the workers at the bottom of the society rebelling
against oppressive conditions. Thus, it was not the White
philanthropists who "freed the slaves." Instead, enslaved
African Americans brought their own liberation "by armed
rebellion, by sullen refusal to work, by poison and murder,
by running away to the North and Canada, by giving point
and powerful example to the agitation of the abolitionists
and by furnishing 200,000 soldiers and many times as many
civilian helpers in the Civil War" (p. 151). Once again, Du
Bois anticipates later historical scholarship that has made it
clear how African Americans have played a central role in
their own social and political liberation. They have been
much more than the "victims" of history.

Du Bois then develops a very strong argument for the
importance of a vital and vibrant multiracial democracy,

one where multiculturalism is prized and fostered. He argues that by leaving out some of the people—as has been done in the partial democracy that is the United States—we leave out "vast stores of wisdom." Only by bringing in the "whole experience" of the human race can societies adequately meet the hard challenges of the unknown future. The expansion of political democracy not only meets the democratic ideals often professed in Western countries, but also makes it likely that much more knowledge and essential wisdom will become available for the long-term development and sustained growth of societies like the United States. The larger the knowledge pool, the more sustainable is the society. Du Bois adds that the expansion of political democracy should be accompanied by the expansion of economic democracy, which he believes workers will increasingly seek. There is much wisdom in the minds of workers and the general public that remains to be tapped.

In chapter 7, "The Damnation of Women," Du Bois yet again shows how much his thinking was ahead of its time. This chapter is one of the first analyses ever by a male intellectual that pressed for greatly expanded women's economic, political, and procreation rights. Du Bois was perhaps the leading male thinker of his day on this subject. He begins this chapter with a highly original analysis of the system of gendered oppression in Western societies like the United States. As he saw the treatment of women in society, they were not really "beings, they were relations." Today as then, women are usually described and positioned by their *relationships* to men—as wives, mothers, daughters, and sisters. Whatever their color, they exist "not for themselves, but for men." Du Bois continues with a brief but insightful analysis of childbearing and child rearing, one that parallels arguments of leading White feminists such as Charlotte

Perkins Gilman: "Only at the sacrifice of intelligence and the chance to do their best work can the majority of modern women bear children. This is the damnation of women" (p. 174). He then adds forcefully and forthrightly that a woman must have control of her own body, the "right of motherhood at her own discretion." Such a view was revolutionary for his time. At an early point in U.S. feminism, this Black male intellectual and activist insisted not only on voting rights for women, a central cause of the period, but also on their economic and procreation rights.

Perhaps most importantly, Du Bois accents in this essay the central role of Black women in Black history and culture, both in African societies and in the United States. He reviews the devastating impact of slavery on these women. The "crushing weight of slavery" means "no legal marriage, no legal family, no legal control over children" (p. 178). He writes provocatively and eloquently on the consequences of slavery: "I shall forgive the white South much in its final judgment day: I shall forgive its slavery, for slavery is a world-old habit; I shall forgive its fighting for a well-lost cause . . . but one thing I shall never forgive, neither in this world nor the world to come: its wanton and continued and persistent insulting of the black womanhood which it sought and seeks to prostitute to its lust" (p. 181). After reviewing the lives and contributions of women such as Harriet Tubman, Phillis Wheatley, Mary Shadd, Louise De Mortie, and Kate Ferguson, Du Bois concludes with a review of the current scene, where Black women are key pillars in the churches and schools that are often the backbone of Black communities. Moreover, anticipating contemporary analyses of the degradation of the "Black body" and of the White beauty myth, Du Bois celebrates the beauty of Black women: "Their beauty,—their dark and mysterious beauty of midnight eyes, crumpled hair, and soft, full-featured faces. . . . No other women on earth could have merged from the hell of force and temptation which once engulfed and still surrounds black women in America with half the modesty and womanliness that they retain" (p. 192).

In chapter 8 Du Bois continues with ever more high-level insights into contemporary societies. In this chapter, titled "The Immortal Child," the focus is on children and education. Du Bois begins with a discussion of the contributions of Europeans and Americans who had mixed White and African ancestry, then moves to a discussion of how Black parents raise their children to prepare them for dealing with racism. This is followed by a probing assessment of the general importance of education. Here he underscores the importance of extended educations for all people, once again making the point that a society cannot afford to ignore the knowledge and wisdom developed by ordinary people. Central to this essay is an insight that others have articulated but few have put so eloquently: "If we realized that children are the future, that immortality is the present child, that no education which educates can possibly be too costly, then we know that the menace of Kaiserism [Germany in World War I] which called for the expenditure of more than 332 thousand millions of dollars was not a whit more pressing than the menace of ignorance, and that no nation tomorrow can call itself civilized which does not give every single human being college and vocational training free and under the best teaching force procurable for love or money" (p. 217). Thinking "outside the box" once again, Du Bois not only recognizes the importance of education for all Americans, including those who are victims of racial oppression, but also accents the importance of a multicultural education that teaches children that racial hatreds not only degrade and kill others, but also "crucify souls like their own." Here, as in chapter 2, Du Bois accents the costs of racism for White Americans. He views comprehensive education across all social lines as one major solution for racial hatreds and oppression. He notes that nowhere in the Western world is education seen this way, an evaluation that still holds true today.

In chapter 9, titled "Of Beauty and Death," Du Bois contrasts the ugliness of racial oppression with the beauty of the physical landscape, using lyrical sentences to describe that landscape. Du Bois raises the question of why those burdened by racism cannot flee to the areas of great natural beauty, and returns with the answer given by Black acquaintances—Jim Crow segregation makes travel too difficult and dangerous. White-generated ugliness can be seen in the blatant Jim Crow segregation of the U.S. Army during the World War I period and in the many racial riots by White Americans against African Americans in that same period. This pain and ugliness is contrasted with the beauty of such physical phenomena as the sunset and moonlight on Montego Bay and with the laughter and loving of African Americans enjoying a Harlem night. "And then—the Veil. It drops as drops the night on southern seas—vast, sudden, unanswering. There is Hate behind it, and Cruelty and Tears. . . . And yet it hangs there, this Veil, between Then and Now, between Pale and Colored and Black and White—between You and Me" (p. 245). Once again, he returns to the metaphor of the veil. African Americans are enshrouded by the veil of White racism.

In chapter 10, titled "The Comet," Du Bois concludes *Darkwater* with a change of pace—a science-fiction parable of chilling relevance to the present day. The tale is set in New York City, whose population is almost entirely wiped out as a comet hits the city. A working-class Black man named Jim is not killed. He is a bank messenger who was saved because he was sent below ground to look at bank records. He comes out into the streets to discover that everyone in sight is dead. As he traverses the city, he rescues a wealthy young White woman, Julia, from an upper floor of her building, where she had been saved because she was in a photographic darkroom when the comet hit. Crossing the city in her luxury car, they find no survivors. Returning to her father's office tower, Jim and Julia go up to the roof to look out over the city. In the face of what appears to be the end of the world, they interact more as human beings than in terms of the social positions they have long inhabited. Commenting on the meaningless-ness of categorizing rich and poor, Julia says, "how foolish our human distinctions seem—now." He replies, "Yes—I was not—human, yesterday." She adds, "And your people were not my people . . . but today—" He adds, "Death, the leveler!" Du Bois then adds the comment that Jim "was no longer a thing apart, a creature below . . . but her Brother Humanity incarnate . . ." (p. 266).

However, as the protagonists move toward each other with outstretched arms, they hear the honking of a car horn below. Soon, two White men come up in the elevator to the roof. One is Julia's father, who tells her that only New York City has been destroyed. Seeing Jim, her father snarls, "It's—a—nigger—Julia! Has he—has he dared—" Julia looks at Jim, drops her eyes, and replies to her father that Jim only dared to rescue her. Then her father throws some money at Jim. A gathering White crowd whispers that they should "lynch the damned—" Someone adds, "Well, what do you think of that? . . . of all New York, just a white girl and a nigger" (p. 270).

Du Bois concludes the chapter and his book with a

poem called "A Hymn to the Peoples," which ends with these words, "Save us, World-Spirit, from our lesser selves! Grant us that war and hatred cease. Reveal our souls in every race and hue! Help us, O Human God, in this Thy Truce, To make Humanity divine!" (pp. 272–73).

Interestingly, most White reviewers of the book could not see past what they viewed as its "hateful" and anti-White stance. They criticized its "bitterness" and its "teaching of violence," neither of which sentiments are to be found in the book. Too tied up in their racial straightjackets, most White readers missed the many astute and consequential points in the book. Moreover, a few reviewers chided Du Bois for writing in language that was above the heads of ordinary Black people, yet they were off the mark. Many ordinary African Americans sent in two dollars to get a copy, much to the amazement of these analysts.[2] Poor and working-class African Americans eagerly sought after a book that, it seems likely, many could barely read. The reason was obvious. Du Bois was now a respected leader of African Americans, and he articulated well the experience and views of most African Americans whatever their social class position.

Du Bois was an authentic American genius. He was a major sociologist and historian, a leading civil rights activist, an essayist, a poet, and a novelist of originality. Viewing his many talents and achievements, it seems that no American has ever contributed so much to his country. As a founder of, and a key innovator in the NAACP (he was founding editor of the *Crisis*), he worked for decades to see the Black civil rights movement rise to power from the 1940s to the 1960s. Indeed, word of his death in Africa came on the day of the most famous civil rights demonstration in U.S. history, the March on Washington in August 1963. In addition, Du Bois pioneered in many areas of social-science scholarship. He undertook the first major research study on the U.S. slave trade (his doctoral dissertation published by Harvard University Press), developed the first book-length urban field study in U.S. social science (*The Philadelphia Negro*), wrote a major revisionist history of Reconstruction (*Black Reconstruction*), developed the first important Whiteness study (chapter 2 here), and wrote much in the way of pathbreaking Pan-Africanist and postcolonial analysis.

Moreover, unlike virtually all White leaders of his day, Du Bois was an active antiracist in thought, writings, and action, and, unlike virtually all male leaders of his day, he was an early and strong feminist. What other American has such a record? Du Bois may well be the greatest American of all time. *Darkwater* repeatedly shows that Du Bois saw much farther and deeper than most contemporaries on matters of what are now called "race, gender, and class." Indeed, many of his insights are *ahead of our time.*

I will conclude this introduction with one of his predictions. After assessing the great destructiveness of World War I—which he sees as substantially an avaricious struggle among European powers for colonial control over the darker peoples of the world—Du Bois boldly anticipates a global war of the races. In this passage from chapter 2, he speaks of the world's majority watching the so-called world war of the Europeans:

> But what of the darker world that watches? Most men belong to this world. With Negro and Negroid, East Indian, Chinese, and Japanese they form two-thirds of the population of the world. A belief in humanity is a belief in colored men. If the uplift of mankind must be done by men, then the destinies of this world will rest ultimately in the hands of darker nations.
>
> What, then, is this dark world thinking? It is think-

ing that as wild and awful as this shameful war was, *it is nothing to compare with that fight for freedom which black and brown and yellow men must and will make unless their oppression and humiliation and insult at the hands of the White World cease. The Dark World is going to submit to its present treatment just as long as it must and not one moment later.* (pp. 71–72, his italics)

Joe R. Feagin
Graduate Research Professor
University of Florida

NOTES

1. W. E. B. Du Bois, *Black Reconstruction in America 1860–1880* (1935; reprint, New York: Atheneum, 1992), p. 10.

2. See the reviews cited in David Levering Lewis, *W. E. B. Du Bois: The Fight for Equality and the American Century, 1919–1963* (New York: Henry Holt, 2000), p. 20.

DARKWATER

AD NINAM

MAY 12, 1896

POSTSCRIPT

These are the things of which men think, who live: of their own selves and the dwelling place of their fathers; of their neighbors; of work and service; of rule and reason and women and children; of Beauty and Death and War. To this thinking I have only to add a point of view: I have been in the world, but not of it. I have seen the human drama from a veiled corner, where all the outer tragedy and comedy have reproduced themselves in microcosm within. From this inner torment of souls the human scene without has interpreted itself to me in unusual and even illuminating ways. For this reason, and this alone, I venture to write again on themes on which great souls have already said greater words, in the hope that I may strike here and there a half-tone, newer even if slighter, up from the heart of my problem and the problems of my people.

Between the sterner flights of logic, I have sought to set some little alightings of what may be poetry. They are tributes to Beauty, unworthy to stand alone; yet perversely, in my mind, now at the end, I know not whether I mean the Thought for the Fancy—or the Fancy for the Thought, or why the book trails off to playing, rather than standing strong on unanswering fact. But this is always—is it not?—the Riddle of Life.

Many of my words appear here transformed from other publications and I thank the *Atlantic*, the *Independent*, the *Crisis*, and the *Journal of Race Development* for letting me use them again.

W. E. BURGHARDT DU BOIS.
New York, 1919.

CONTENTS

CREDO

I believe in God, who made of one blood all nations that on earth do dwell. I believe that all men, black and brown and white, are brothers, varying through time and opportunity, in form and gift and feature, but differing in no essential particular, and alike in soul and the possibility of infinite development.

Especially do I believe in the Negro Race: in the beauty of its genius, the sweetness of its soul, and its strength in that meekness which shall yet inherit this turbulent earth.

I believe in Pride of race and lineage and self: in pride of self so deep as to scorn injustice to other selves; in pride of lineage so great as to despise no man's father; in pride of race so chivalrous as neither to offer bastardy to the weak nor beg wedlock of the strong, knowing that men may be brothers in Christ, even though they be not brothers-in-law.

I believe in Service—humble, reverent service, from the blackening of boots to the whitening of souls; for Work is Heaven, Idleness Hell, and Wage is the "Well done!" of the Master, who summoned all them that labor and are heavy laden, making no distinction between the black, sweating cotton hands of Georgia and the first families of Virginia, since all distinction not based on deed is devilish and not divine.

I believe in the Devil and his angels, who wantonly work to narrow the opportunity of struggling human beings, especially if they be black; who spit in the faces of the fallen, strike them that cannot strike again, believe the worst and work to prove it, hating the image which their Maker stamped on a brother's soul.

I believe in the Prince of Peace. I believe that War is Murder. I believe that armies and navies are at bottom the tinsel and braggadocio of oppression and wrong, and I believe that the wicked conquest of weaker and darker nations by nations whiter and stronger but foreshadows the death of that strength.

I believe in Liberty for all men: the space to stretch their arms and their souls, the right to breathe and the right to vote, the freedom to choose their friends, enjoy the sunshine, and ride on the railroads, uncursed by color; thinking, dreaming, working as they will in a kingdom of beauty and love.

I believe in the Training of Children, black even as white; the leading out of little souls into the green pastures and beside the still waters, not for pelf or peace, but for life lit by some large vision of beauty and goodness and truth; lest we forget, and the sons of the fathers, like Esau, for mere meat barter their birthright in a mighty nation.

Finally, I believe in Patience—patience with the weakness of the Weak and the strength of the Strong, the prejudice of the Ignorant and the ignorance of the Blind; patience with the tardy triumph of Joy and the mad chastening of Sorrow;—patience with God!

I | THE SHADOW OF YEARS

I was born by a golden river and in the shadow of two great hills, five years after the Emancipation Proclamation. The house was quaint, with clapboards running up and down, neatly trimmed, and there were five rooms, a tiny porch, a rosy front yard, and unbelievably delicious strawberries in the rear. A South Carolinian, lately come to the Berkshire Hills, owned all this—tall, thin, and black, with golden earrings, and given to religious trances. We were his transient tenants for the time.

My own people were part of a great clan. Fully two hundred years before, Tom Burghardt had come through the western pass from the Hudson with his Dutch captor, "Coenraet Burghardt," sullen in his slavery and achieving his freedom by volunteering for the Revolution at a time of sudden alarm. His wife was a little, black, Bantu woman, who never became reconciled to this strange land; she clasped her knees and rocked and crooned:

"Do bana coba—gene me, gene me!
Ben d'nuli, ben d'le—"

Tom died about 1787, but of him came many sons, and one, Jack, who helped in the War of 1812. Of Jack and his wife, Violet, was born a mighty family, splendidly named: Harlow and Ira, Cloë, Lucinda, Maria, and Othello! I dimly remember my grandfather, Othello,—or "Uncle Tallow,"— a brown man, strong-voiced and redolent with tobacco, who sat stiffly in a great high chair because his hip was broken. He was probably a bit lazy and given to wassail. At any rate, grandmother had a shrewish tongue and often berated him. This grandmother was Sarah—"Aunt Sally"— a stern, tall, Dutch-African woman, beak-nosed, but beautiful-eyed and golden-skinned. Ten or more children were theirs, of whom the youngest was Mary, my mother.

Mother was dark shining bronze, with a tiny ripple in her black hair, black-eyed, with a heavy, kind face. She gave one the impression of infinite patience, but a curious determination was concealed in her softness. The family were small farmers on Egremont Plain, between Great Barrington and Sheffield, Massachusetts. The bits of land were too small to support the great families born on them and we were always poor. I never remember being cold or hungry, but I do remember that shoes and coal, and sometimes flour, caused mother moments of anxious thought in winter, and a new suit was an event!

At about the time of my birth economic pressure was transmuting the family generally from farmers to "hired" help. Some revolted and migrated westward, others went cityward as cooks and barbers. Mother worked for some years at house service in Great Barrington, and after a disappointed love episode with a cousin, who went to California, she met and married Alfred Du Bois and went to town to live by the golden river where I was born.

Alfred, my father, must have seemed a splendid vision in

that little valley under the shelter of those mighty hills. He was small and beautiful of face and feature, just tinted with the sun, his curly hair chiefly revealing his kinship to Africa. In nature he was a dreamer,—romantic, indolent, kind, unreliable. He had in him the making of a poet, an adventurer, or a Beloved Vagabond, according to the life that closed round him; and that life gave him all too little. His father, Alexander Du Bois, cloaked under a stern, austere demeanor a passionate revolt against the world. He, too, was small, but squarish. I remember him as I saw him first, in his home in New Bedford,—white hair close-cropped; a seamed, hard face, but high in tone, with a gray eye that could twinkle or glare.

Long years before him Louis XIV drove two Huguenots, Jacques and Louis Du Bois, into wild Ulster County, New York. One of them in the third or fourth generation had a descendant, Dr. James Du Bois, a gay, rich bachelor, who made his money in the Bahamas, where he and the Gilberts had plantations. There he took a beautiful little mulatto slave as his mistress, and two sons were born: Alexander in 1803 and John, later. They were fine, straight, clear-eyed boys, white enough to "pass." He brought them to America and put Alexander in the celebrated Cheshire School, in Connecticut. Here he often visited him, but one last time, fell dead. He left no will, and his relations made short shrift of these sons. They gathered in the property, apprenticed grandfather to a shoemaker; then dropped him.

Grandfather took his bitter dose like a thoroughbred. Wild as was his inner revolt against this treatment, he uttered no word against the thieves and made no plea. He tried his fortunes here and in Haiti, where, during his short, restless sojourn, my own father was born. Eventually, grandfather became chief steward on the passenger boat between

New York and New Haven; later he was a small merchant
in Springfield; and finally he retired and ended his days at
New Bedford. Always he held his head high, took no
insults, made few friends. He was not a "Negro"; he was a
man! Yet the current was too strong even for him. Then
even more than now a colored man had colored friends or
none at all, lived in a colored world or lived alone. A few
fine, strong, black men gained the heart of this silent, bitter
man in New York and New Haven. If he had scant sympathy with their social clannishness, he was with them in
fighting discrimination. So, when the white Episcopalians
of Trinity Parish, New Haven, showed plainly that they no
longer wanted black folk as fellow Christians, he led the
revolt which resulted in St. Luke's Parish, and was for years
its senior warden. He lies dead in the Grove Street Ceme-
tery, beside Jehudi Ashmun.

Beneath his sternness was a very human man. Slyly he
wrote poetry,—stilted, pleading things from a soul astray.
He loved women in his masterful way, marrying three beautiful wives in succession and clinging to each with a certain
desperate, even if unsympathetic, affection. As a father he
was, naturally, a failure,—hard, domineering, unyielding.
His four children reacted characteristically: one was until
past middle life a thin spinster, the mental image of her
father; one died; one passed over into the white world and
her children's children are now white, with no knowledge
of their Negro blood; the fourth, my father, bent before
grandfather, but did not break—better if he had. He yielded
and flared back, asked forgiveness and forgot why, became
the harshly-held favorite, who ran away and rioted and
roamed and loved and married my brown mother.

So with some circumstance having finally gotten myself
born, with a flood of Negro blood, a strain of French, a bit

of Dutch, but, thank God! no "Anglo-Saxon," I come to the days of my childhood.

They were very happy. Early we moved back to Grandfather Burghardt's home,—I barely remember its stone fireplace, big kitchen, and delightful woodshed. Then this house passed to other branches of the clan and we moved to rented quarters in town,—to one delectable place "upstairs," with a wide yard full of shrubbery, and a brook; to another house abutting a railroad, with infinite interests and astonishing playmates; and finally back to the quiet street on which I was born,—down a long lane and in a homely, cozy cottage, with a living-room, a tiny sitting-room, a pantry, and two attic bedrooms. Here mother and I lived until she died, in 1884, for father early began his restless wanderings. I last remember urgent letters for us to come to New Milford, where he had started a barber shop. Later he became a preacher. But mother no longer trusted his dreams, and he soon faded out of our lives into silence.

From the age of five until I was sixteen I went to school on the same grounds,—down a lane, into a widened yard, with a big choke-cherry tree and two buildings, wood and brick. Here I got acquainted with my world, and soon had my criterions of judgment.

Wealth had no particular lure. On the other hand, the shadow of wealth was about us. That river of my birth was golden because of the woolen and paper waste that soiled it. The gold was theirs, not ours; but the gleam and glint was for all. To me it was all in order and I took it philosophically. I cordially despised the poor Irish and South Germans, who slaved in the mills, and annexed the rich and well-to-do as my natural companions. Of such is the kingdom of snobs!

Most of our townfolk were, naturally, the well-to-do,

shading downward, but seldom reaching poverty. As play-
mate of the children I saw the homes of nearly every one,
except a few immigrant New Yorkers, of whom none of us
approved. The homes I saw impressed me, but did not overwhelm me. Many were bigger than mine, with newer and
shinier things, but they did not seem to differ in kind. I
think I probably surprised my hosts more than they me, for
I was easily at home and perfectly happy and they looked to
me just like ordinary people, while my brown face and frizzled hair must have seemed strange to them.

Yet I was very much one of them. I was a center and
sometimes the leader of the town gang of boys. We were
noisy, but never very bad,—and, indeed, my mother's quiet
influence came in here, as I realize now. She did not try to
make me perfect. To her I was already perfect. She simply
warned me of a few things, especially saloons. In my town
the saloon was the open door to hell. The best families had
their drunkards and the worst had little else.

Very gradually,—I cannot now distinguish the steps,
though here and there I remember a jump or a jolt—but
very gradually I found myself assuming quite placidly that I
was different from other children. At first I think I con-
nected the difference with a manifest ability to get my
lessons rather better than most and to recite with a certain
happy, almost taunting, glibness, which brought frowns here
and there. Then, slowly, I realized that some folks, a few,
even several, actually considered my brown skin a misfortune; once or twice I became painfully aware that some
human beings even thought it a crime. I was not for a
moment daunted,—although, of course, there were some
days of secret tears—rather I was spurred to tireless effort. If
they beat me at anything, I was grimly determined to make
them sweat for it! Once I remember challenging a great,

hard farmer-boy to battle, when I knew he could whip me; and he did. But ever after, he was polite.

As time flew I felt not so much disowned and rejected as rather drawn up into higher spaces and made part of a mightier mission. At times I almost pitied my pale companions, who were not of the Lord's anointed and who saw in their dreams no splendid quests of golden fleeces.

Even in the matter of girls my peculiar phantasy asserted itself. Naturally, it was in our town voted bad form for boys of twelve and fourteen to show any evident weakness for girls. We tolerated them loftily, and now and then they played in our games, when I joined in quite as naturally as the rest. It was when strangers came, or summer boarders, or when the oldest girls grew up that my sharp senses noted little hesitancies in public and searchings for possible public opinion. Then I flamed! I lifted my chin and strode off to the mountains, where I viewed the world at my feet and strained my eyes across the shadow of the hills.

I was graduated from high school at sixteen, and I talked of "Wendell Phillips." This was my first sweet taste of the world's applause. There were flowers and upturned faces, music and marching, and there was my mother's smile. She was lame, then, and a bit drawn, but very happy. It was her great day and that very year she lay down with a sigh of content and has not yet awakened. I felt a certain gladness to see her, at last, at peace, for she had worried all her life. Of my own loss I had then little realization. That came only with the after-years. Now it was the choking gladness and solemn feel of wings! At last, I was going beyond the hills and into the world that beckoned steadily.

There came a little pause,—a singular pause. I was given to understand that I was almost too young for the world. Harvard was the goal of my dreams, but my white friends hesitated and my colored friends were silent. Harvard was a mighty conjure-word in that hill town, and even the mill owners' sons had aimed lower. Finally it was tactfully explained that the place for me was in the South among my people. A scholarship had been already arranged at Fisk, and my summer earnings would pay the fare. My relatives grumbled, but after a twinge I felt a strange delight! I forgot, or did not thoroughly realize, the curious irony by which I was not looked upon as a real citizen of my birth-town, with a future and a career, and instead was being sent to a far land among strangers who were regarded as (and in truth were) "mine own people."

Ah! the wonder of that journey, with its faint spice of adventure, as I entered the land of slaves; the never-to-be-forgotten marvel of that first supper at Fisk with the world "colored" and opposite two of the most beautiful beings God ever revealed to the eyes of seventeen. I promptly lost my appetite, but I was deliriously happy!

As I peer back through the shadow of my years, seeing not too clearly, but through the thickening veil of wish and after-thought, I seem to view my life divided into four distinct parts: the Age of Miracles, the Days of Disillusion, the Discipline of Work and Play, and the Second Miracle Age.

The Age of Miracles began with Fisk and ended with Germany. I was bursting with the joy of living. I seemed to ride in conquering might. I was captain of my soul and master of fate! I *willed* to do! It was done. I *wished*! The wish came true.

Now and then out of the void flashed the great sword of hate to remind me of the battle. I remember once, in Nashville, brushing by accident against a white woman on the street. Politely and eagerly I raised my hat to apologize. That was thirty-five years ago. From that day to this I have never knowingly raised my hat to a Southern white woman.

I suspect that beneath all of my seeming triumphs there were many failures and disappointments, but the realities loomed so large that they swept away even the memory of other dreams and wishes. Consider, for a moment, how miraculous it all was to a boy of seventeen, just escaped from a narrow valley: I willed and lo! my people came dancing about me,—riotous in color, gay in laughter, full of sympathy, need, and pleading; darkly delicious girls—"colored" girls—sat beside me and actually talked to me while I gazed in tongue-tied silence or babbled in boastful dreams. Boys with my own experiences and out of my own world, who knew and understood, wrought out with me great remedies. I studied eagerly under teachers who bent in subtle sympathy, feeling themselves some shadow of the Veil and lifting it gently that we darker souls might peer through to other worlds.

I willed and lo! I was walking beneath the elms of Harvard,—the name of allurement, the college of my youngest, wildest visions! I needed money; scholarships and prizes fell into my lap,—not all I wanted or strove for, but all I needed to keep in school. Commencement came and standing before governor, president, and grave, gowned men, I told them certain astonishing truths, waving my arms and breathing fast! They applauded with what now seems to me uncalled-for fervor, but then! I walked home on pink clouds of glory! I asked for a fellowship and got it. I announced my plan of studying in Germany, but Harvard had no more fellowships for me. A friend, however, told me of the Slater Fund and how the Board was looking for colored men worth educating. No thought of modest hesitation occurred to me. I rushed at the chance.

The trustees of the Slater Fund excused themselves politely. They acknowledged that they had in the past looked for colored boys of ability to educate, but, being unsuccessful, they had stopped searching. I went at them hammer and tongs! I plied them with testimonials and mid-year and final marks. I intimated plainly, impudently, that they were "stalling"! In vain did the chairman, Ex-President Hayes, explain and excuse. I took no excuses and brushed explanations aside. I wonder now that he did not brush me aside, too, as a conceited meddler, but instead he smiled and surrendered.

I crossed the ocean in a trance. Always I seemed to be saying, "It is not real; I must be dreaming!" I can live it again—the little, Dutch ship—the blue waters—the smell of new-mown hay—Holland and the Rhine. I saw the Wartburg and Berlin; I made the Harzreise and climbed the Brocken; I saw the Hansa towns and the cities and dorfs of South Germany; I saw the Alps at Berne, the Cathedral at Milan, Florence, Rome, Venice, Vienna, and Pesth; I looked on the boundaries of Russia; and I sat in Paris and London.

On mountain and valley, in home and school, I met men and women as I had never met them before. Slowly they became, not white folks, but folks. The unity beneath all life clutched me. I was not less fanatically a Negro, but "Negro" meant a greater, broader sense of humanity and world-fellowship. I felt myself standing, not against the world, but simply against American narrowness and color prejudice, with the greater, finer world at my back urging me on.

I builded great castles in Spain and lived therein. I dreamed and loved and wandered and sang; then, after two long years, I dropped suddenly back into "nigger"-hating America!

My Days of Disillusion were not disappointing enough to discourage me. I was still upheld by that fund of infinite faith, although dimly about me I saw the shadow of disaster. I began to realize how much of what I had called Will and

Ability was sheer Luck! *Suppose* my good mother had pre-
ferred a steady income from my child labor rather than bank
on the precarious dividend of my higher training? *Suppose*
that pompous old village judge, whose dignity we often ruf-
fled and whose apples we stole, had had his way and sent me
while a child to a "reform" school to learn a "trade"? *Suppose*
Principal Hosmer had been born with no faith in "darkies,"
and instead of giving me Greek and Latin had taught me
carpentry and the making of tin pans? *Suppose* I had missed
a Harvard scholarship? *Suppose* the Slater Board had then, as
now, distinct ideas as to where the education of Negroes
should stop? Suppose *and* suppose! As I sat down calmly on
flat earth and looked at my life a certain great fear seized me.
Was I the masterful captain or the pawn of laughing sprites?
Who was I to fight a world of color prejudice? I raise my hat
to myself when I remember that, even with these thoughts,
I did not hesitate or waver; but just went doggedly to work,
and therein lay whatever salvation I have achieved.

First came the task of earning a living. I was not nice or
hard to please. I just got down on my knees and begged for
work, anything and anywhere. I wrote to Hampton,
Tuskegee, and a dozen other places. They politely declined,
with many regrets. The trustees of a backwoods Tennessee
town considered me, but were eventually afraid. Then, suddenly, Wilberforce offered to let me teach Latin and Greek
at $750 a year. I was overjoyed!

I did not know anything about Latin and Greek, but I
did know of Wilberforce. The breath of that great name
had swept the water and dropped into southern Ohio,
where Southerners had taken their cure at Tawawa Springs
and where white Methodists had planted a school; then
came the little bishop, Daniel Payne, who made it a school
of the African Methodists. This was the school that called

me, and when re-considered offers from Tuskegee and Jefferson City followed, I refused; I was so thankful for that first offer.

I went to Wilberforce with high ideals. I wanted to help to build a great university. I was willing to work night as well as day. I taught Latin, Greek, English, and German. I helped in the discipline, took part in the social life, begged to be allowed to lecture on sociology, and began to write books. But I found myself against a stone wall. Nothing stirred before my impatient pounding! Or if it stirred, it soon slept again.

Of course, I was too impatient! The snarl of years was not to be undone in days. I set at solving the problem before I knew it. Wilberforce was a colored church-school. In it were mingled the problems of poorly-prepared pupils, an inadequately-equipped plant, the natural politics of bishoprics, and the provincial reactions of a country town loaded with traditions. It was my first introduction to a Negro world, and I was at once marvelously inspired and deeply depressed. I was inspired with the children,—had I not rubbed against the children of the world and did I not find here the same eagerness, the same joy of life, the same brains as in New England, France, and Germany? But, on the other hand, the ropes and myths and knots and hindrances; the thundering waves of the white world beyond beating us back; the scalding breakers of this inner world,— its currents and back eddies—its meanness and smallness— its sorrow and tragedy—its screaming farce!

In all this I was as one bound hand and foot. Struggle, work, fight as I would, I seemed to get nowhere and accomplish nothing. I had all the wild intolerance of youth, and no experience in human tangles. For the first time in my life I realized that there were limits to my will to do.

The Day of Miracles was past, and a long, gray road of dogged work lay ahead.

I had, naturally, my triumphs here and there. I defied the bishops in the matter of public extemporaneous prayer and they yielded. I bearded the poor, hunted president in his den, and yet was re-elected to my position. I was slowly winning a way, but quickly losing faith in the value of the way won. Was this the place to begin my life work? Was this the work which I was best fitted to do? What business had I, anyhow, to teach Greek when I had studied men? I grew sure that I had made a mistake. So I determined to leave Wilberforce and try elsewhere. Thus, the third period of my life began.

First, in 1896, I married—a slip of a girl, beautifully dark-eyed and thorough and good as a German housewife. Then I accepted a job to make a study of Negroes in Philadelphia for the University of Pennsylvania,—one year at six hundred dollars. How did I dare these two things? I do not know. Yet they spelled salvation. To remain at Wilberforce without doing my ideals meant spiritual death. Both my wife and I were homeless. I dared a home and a temporary job. But it was a different daring from the days of my first youth. I was ready to admit that the best of men might fail. I meant still to be captain of my soul, but I realized that even captains are not omnipotent in uncharted and angry seas.

I essayed a thorough piece of work in Philadelphia. I labored morning, noon, and night. Nobody ever reads that fat volume on "The Philadelphia Negro," but they treat it with respect, and that consoles me. The colored people of Philadelphia received me with no open arms. They had a natural dislike to being studied like a strange species. I met again and in different guise those curious cross-currents and inner social whirlings of my own people. They set me to groping. I concluded that I did not know so much as I might about my own people, and when President Bumstead invited me to Atlanta University the next year to teach sociology and study the American Negro, I accepted gladly, at a salary of twelve hundred dollars.

My real life work was done at Atlanta for thirteen years, from my twenty-ninth to my forty-second birthday. They were years of great spiritual upturning, of the making and unmaking of ideals, of hard work and hard play. Here I found myself. I lost most of my mannerisms. I grew more broadly human, made my closest and most holy friendships, and studied human beings. I became widely-acquainted with the real condition of my people. I realized the terrific odds which faced them. At Wilberforce I was their captious critic. In Philadelphia I was their cold and scientific investigator, with microscope and probe. It took but a few years of Atlanta to bring me to hot and indignant defense. I saw the race-hatred of the whites as I had never dreamed of it before,—naked and unashamed! The faint discrimination of my hopes and intangible dislikes paled into nothing before this great, red monster of cruel oppression. I held back with more difficulty each day my mounting indignation against injustice and misrepresentation.

With all this came the strengthening and hardening of my own character. The billows of birth, love, and death swept over me. I saw life through all its paradox and contradiction of streaming eyes and mad merriment. I emerged into full manhood, with the ruins of some ideals about me, but with others planted above the stars; scarred and a bit grim, but hugging to my soul the divine gift of laughter and withal determined, even unto stubbornness, to fight the good fight.

At last, forbear and waver as I would, I faced the great Decision. My life's last and greatest door stood ajar. What with all my dreaming, studying, and teaching was I going to *do* in this fierce fight? Despite all my youthful conceit and bumptiousness, I found developed beneath it all a reticence and new fear of forwardness, which sprang from searching criticisms of motive and high ideals of efficiency; but contrary to my dream of racial solidarity and notwithstanding my deep desire to serve and follow and think, rather than to lead and inspire and decide, I found myself suddenly the leader of a great wing of people fighting against another and greater wing.

Nor could any effort of mine keep this fight from sinking to the personal plane. Heaven knows I tried. That first meeting of a knot of enthusiasts, at Niagara Falls, had all the earnestness of self-devotion. At the second meeting, at Harper's Ferry, it arose to the solemnity of a holy crusade and yet without and to the cold, hard stare of the world it seemed merely the envy of fools against a great man, Booker Washington.

Of the movement I was willy-nilly leader. I hated the rôle. For the first time I faced criticism and *cared*. Every ideal and habit of my life was cruelly misjudged. I who had always overstriven to give credit for good work, who had never consciously stooped to envy was accused by honest colored people of every sort of small and petty jealousy, while white people said I was ashamed of my race and wanted to be white! And this of me, whose one life fanaticism had been belief in my Negro blood!

Away back in the little years of my boyhood I had sold the Springfield *Republican* and written for Mr. Fortune's *Globe*. I dreamed of being an editor myself some day. I am an editor. In the great, slashing days of college life I dreamed of a strong organization to fight the battles of the

Negro race. The National Association for the Advancement of Colored People is such a body, and it grows daily. In the dark days at Wilberforce I planned a time when I could speak freely to my people and of them, interpreting between two worlds. I am speaking now. In the study at Atlanta I grew to fear lest my radical beliefs should so hurt the college that either my silence or the institution's ruin would result. Powers and principalities have not yet curbed my tongue and Atlanta still lives.

It all came—this new Age of Miracles—because a few persons in 1909 determined to celebrate Lincoln's Birthday properly by calling for the final emancipation of the American Negro. I came at their call. My salary even for a year was not assured, but it was the "Voice without reply." The result has been the National Association for the Advancement of Colored People and *The Crisis* and this book, which I am finishing on my Fiftieth Birthday.

Last year I looked death in the face and found its lineaments not unkind. But it was not my time. Yet in nature some time soon and in the fullness of days I shall die, quietly, I trust, with my face turned South and eastward; and, dreaming or dreamless, I shall, I am sure, enjoy death as I have enjoyed life.

A Litany at Atlanta

O Silent God, Thou whose voice afar in mist and mystery hath left our ears an-hungered in these fearful days—

Hear us, good Lord!

Listen to us, Thy children: our faces dark with doubt are made a mockery in Thy Sanctuary. With uplifted hands we front Thy Heaven, O God, crying:

We beseech Thee to hear us, good Lord!

We are not better than our fellows, Lord; we are but weak and human men. When our devils do deviltry, curse Thou the doer and the deed,—curse them as we curse them, do to them all and more than ever they have done to innocence and weakness, to womanhood and home.

Have mercy upon us, miserable sinners!

And yet, whose is the deeper guilt? Who made these devils? Who nursed them in crime and fed them on injustice? Who ravished and debauched their mothers and their grandmothers? Who bought and sold their crime and waxed fat and rich on public iniquity?

Thou knowest, good God!

Is this Thy Justice, O Father, that guile be easier than innocence and the innocent be crucified for the guilt of the untouched guilty?

Justice, O Judge of men!

Wherefore do we pray? Is not the God of the Fathers dead? Have not seers seen in Heaven's halls Thine hearsed

51

and lifeless form stark amidst the black and rolling smoke of sin, where all along bow bitter forms of endless dead?

Awake, Thou that sleepest!

Thou art not dead, but flown afar, up hills of endless light, through blazing corridors of suns, where worlds do swing of good and gentle men, of women strong and free— far from the cozenage, black hypocrisy, and chaste prostitution of this shameful speck of dust!

Turn again, O Lord; leave us not to perish in our sin!

From lust of body and lust of blood,—

Great God, deliver us!

From lust of power and lust of gold,—

Great God, deliver us!

From the leagued lying of despot and of brute,—

Great God, deliver us!

A city lay in travail, God our Lord, and from her loins sprang twin Murder and Black Hate. Red was the midnight; clang, crack, and cry of death and fury filled the air and trembled underneath the stars where church spires pointed silently to Thee. And all this was to sate the greed of greedy men who hide behind the veil of vengeance!

Bend us Thine ear, O Lord!

In the pale, still morning we looked upon the deed. We stopped our ears and held our leaping hands, but they—did they not wag their heads and leer and cry with bloody jaws: *Cease from Crime!* The word was mockery, for thus they train a hundred crimes while we do cure one.

Turn again our captivity, O Lord!

Behold this maimed and broken thing, dear God; it was an humble black man, who toiled and sweat to save a bit from the pittance paid him. They told him: *Work and Rise!* He worked. Did this man sin? Nay, but someone told how someone said another did—one whom he had never seen nor known. Yet for that man's crime this man lieth maimed and murdered, his wife naked to shame, his children to poverty and evil.

Hear us, O heavenly Father!

Doth not this justice of hell stink in Thy nostrils, O God? How long shall the mounting flood of innocent blood roar in Thine ears and pound in our hearts for vengeance? Pile the pale frenzy of blood-crazed brutes, who do such deeds, high on Thine Altar, Jehovah Jireh, and burn it in hell forever and forever!

Forgive us, good Lord; we know not what we say!

Bewildered we are and passion-tossed, mad with the madness of a mobbed and mocked and murdered people; straining at the armposts of Thy throne, we raise our shackled hands and charge Thee, God, by the bones of our stolen fathers, by the tears of our dead mothers, by the very blood of Thy crucified Christ: What meaneth this? Tell us the plan; give us the sign!

Keep not Thou silent, O God!

Sit not longer blind, Lord God, deaf to our prayer and dumb to our dumb suffering. Surely Thou, too, art not white, O Lord, a pale, bloodless, heartless thing!

Ah! Christ of all the Pities!

Forgive the thought! Forgive these wild, blasphemous words! Thou art still the God of our black fathers and in Thy Soul's Soul sit some soft darkenings of the evening, some shadowings of the velvet night.

But whisper—speak—call, great God, for Thy silence is white terror to our hearts! The way, O God, show us the way and point us the path!

Whither? North is greed and South is blood; within, the coward, and without, the liar. Whither? To death?

Amen! Welcome, dark sleep!

Whither? To life? But not this life, dear God, not this. Let the cup pass from us, tempt us not beyond our strength, for there is that clamoring and clawing within, to whose voice we would not listen, yet shudder lest we must,—and it is red. Ah! God! It is a red and awful shape.

Selah!

In yonder East trembles a star.

Vengeance is Mine; I will repay, saith the Lord!

Thy Will, O Lord, be done!

Kyrie Eleison!

Lord, we have done these pleading, wavering words.

We beseech Thee to hear us, good Lord!

We bow our heads and hearken soft to the sobbing of women and little children.

We beseech Thee to hear us, good Lord!

Our voices sink in silence and in night.

Hear us, good Lord!

In night, O God of a godless land!

Amen!

In silence, O Silent God.

Selah!

II THE SOULS OF WHITE FOLK

High in the tower, where I sit above the loud complaining of the human sea, I know many souls that toss and whirl and pass, but none there are that intrigue me more than the Souls of White Folk.

Of them I am singularly clairvoyant. I see in and through them. I view them from unusual points of vantage. Not as a foreigner do I come, for I am native, not foreign, bone of their thought and flesh of their language. Mine is not the knowledge of the traveler or the colonial composite of dear memories, words and wonder. Nor yet is my knowledge that which servants have of masters, or mass of class, or capitalist of artisan. Rather I see these souls undressed and from the back and side. I see the working of their entrails. I know their thoughts and they know that I know. This knowledge makes them now embarrassed, now furious! They deny my right to live and be and call me misbirth! My word is to them mere bitterness and my soul, pessimism. And yet as they preach and strut and shout and threaten, crouching as they clutch at rags of facts and fancies to hide their nakedness, they go twisting, flying by my tired eyes and I see them ever stripped,—ugly, human.

The discovery of personal whiteness among the world's peoples is a very modern thing,—a nineteenth and twentieth century matter, indeed. The ancient world would have laughed at such a distinction. The Middle Age regarded skin color with mild curiosity; and even up into the eighteenth century we were hammering our national manikins into one, great, Universal Man, with fine frenzy which ignored color and race even more than birth. Today we have changed all that, and the world in a sudden, emotional conversion has discovered that it is white and by that token, wonderful!

This assumption that of all the hues of God whiteness alone is inherently and obviously better than brownness or tan leads to curious acts; even the sweeter souls of the dominant world as they discourse with me on weather, weal, and woe are continually playing above their actual words an obligato of tune and tone, saying:

"My poor, un-white thing! Weep not nor rage. I know, too well, that the curse of God lies heavy on you. Why? That is not for me to say, but be brave! Do your work in your lowly sphere, praying the good Lord that into heaven above, where all is love, you may, one day, be born—white!"

I do not laugh. I am quite straight-faced as I ask soberly:

"But what on earth is whiteness that one should so desire it?" Then always, somehow, some way, silently but clearly, I am given to understand that whiteness is the ownership of the earth forever and ever, Amen!

Now what is the effect on a man or a nation when it comes passionately to believe such an extraordinary dictum as this? That nations are coming to believe it is manifest daily. Wave on wave, each with increasing virulence, is dashing this new religion of whiteness on the shores of our time. Its first effects are funny: the strut of the Southerner, the arrogance of the Englishman amuck, the whoop of the hoodlum who vicariously leads your mob. Next it appears dampening generous enthusiasm in what we once counted glorious; to free the slave is discovered to be tolerable only in so far as it freed his master! Do we sense somnolent writhings in black Africa or angry groans in India or triumphant banzais in Japan? "To your tents, O Israel!" These nations are not white!

After the more comic manifestations and the chilling of generous enthusiasm come subtler, darker deeds. Everything considered, the title to the universe claimed by White Folk is faulty. It ought, at least, to look plausible. How easy, then, by emphasis and omission to make children believe that every great soul the world ever saw was a white man's soul; that every great thought the world ever knew was a white man's thought; that every great deed the world ever did was a white man's deed; that every great dream the world ever sang was a white man's dream. In fine, that if from the world were dropped everything that could not fairly be attributed to White Folk, the world would, if anything, be even greater, truer, better than now. And if all this be a lie, is it not a lie in a great cause?

Here it is that the comedy verges to tragedy. The first minor note is struck, all unconsciously, by those worthy souls in whom consciousness of high descent brings burning desire to spread the gift abroad,—the obligation of nobility to the ignoble. Such sense of duty assumes two things: a real possession of the heritage and its frank appreciation by the humble-born. So long, then, as humble black folk, voluble with thanks, receive barrels of old clothes from lordly and generous whites, there is much mental peace and moral satisfaction. But when the black man begins to dispute the white man's title to certain alleged bequests of the Fathers in wage and position, authority and training; and when his attitude toward charity is sullen anger rather than humble jollity; when he insists on his human right to swagger and swear and waste,—then the spell is suddenly broken and the philanthropist is ready to believe that Negroes are impudent, that the South is right, and that Japan wants to fight America.

After this the descent to Hell is easy. On the pale, white faces which the great billows whirl upward to my tower I see again and again, often and still more often, a writing of human hatred, a deep and passionate hatred, vast by the very vagueness of its expressions. Down through the green waters, on the bottom of the world, where men move to and fro, I have seen a man—an educated gentleman—grow livid with anger because a little, silent, black woman was sitting by herself in a Pullman car. He was a white man. I have seen a great, grown man curse a little child, who had wandered into the wrong waiting-room, searching for its mother: "Here, you damned black ————" He was white. In Central Park I have seen the upper lip of a quiet, peaceful man curl back in a tigerish snarl of rage because black folk rode by in a motor car. He was a white man. We have seen, you and I, city after city drunk and furious with ungovernable lust of blood; mad with murder, destroying, killing, and cursing; torturing human victims because somebody accused of crime happened to be of the same color as the mob's innocent victims and because that color was not white! We have seen,—Merciful God! in these wild days and in the name of Civilization, Justice, and Motherhood,—what have we not seen, right here in America, of orgy, cruelty, barbarism, and murder done to men and women of Negro descent.

Up through the foam of green and weltering waters wells this great mass of hatred, in wilder, fiercer violence, until I look down and know that today to the millions of my people no misfortune could happen,—of death and pestilence, failure and defeat—that would not make the hearts of millions of their fellows beat with fierce, vindictive joy! Do you doubt it? Ask your own soul what it would say if the next census were to report that half of black America was dead and the other half dying.

Unfortunate? Unfortunate. But where is the misfortune? Mine? Am I, in my blackness, the sole sufferer? I suffer. And yet, somehow, above the suffering, above the shackled anger that beats the bars, above the hurt that crazes there surges in me a vast pity,—pity for a people imprisoned and enthralled, hampered and made miserable for such a cause, for such a phantasy!

Conceive this nation, of all human peoples, engaged in a crusade to make the "World Safe for Democracy"! Can you imagine the United States protesting against Turkish atrocities in Armenia, while the Turks are silent about mobs in Chicago and St. Louis; what is Louvain compared with Memphis, Waco, Washington, Dyersburg, and Estill Springs? In short, what is the black man but America's Belgium, and how could America condemn in Germany that which she commits, just as brutally, within her own borders?

A true and worthy ideal frees and uplifts a people; a false ideal imprisons and lowers. Say to men, earnestly and repeatedly: "Honesty is best, knowledge is power; do unto others as you would be done by." Say this and act it and the nation must move toward it, if not to it. But say to a people: "The one virtue is to be white," and the people rush to the inevitable conclusion, "Kill the 'nigger'!"

Is not this the record of present America? Is not this its headlong progress? Are we not coming more and more, day by day, to making the statement "I am white," the one fun-

damental tenet of our practical morality? Only when this
basic, iron rule is involved is our defense of right nation-
wide and prompt. Murder may swagger, theft may rule and
prostitution may flourish and the nation gives but spasmodic,
intermittent and lukewarm attention. But let the murderer
be black or the thief brown or the violator of womanhood
have a drop of Negro blood, and the righteousness of the
indignation sweeps the world. Nor would this fact make the
indignation less justifiable did not we all know that it was
blackness that was condemned and not crime.

In the awful cataclysm of World War, where from
beating, slandering, and murdering us the white world
turned temporarily aside to kill each other, we of the
Darker Peoples looked on in mild amaze.

Among some of us, I doubt not, this sudden descent of
Europe into hell brought unbounded surprise; to others,
over wide area, it brought the *Schaden Freude* of the bitterly
hurt; but most of us, I judge, looked on silently and sor-
rowfully, in sober thought, seeing sadly the prophecy of our
own souls.

Here is a civilization that has boasted much. Neither
Roman nor Arab, Greek nor Egyptian, Persian nor Mongol
ever took himself and his own perfectness with such dis-
concerting seriousness as the modern white man. We
whose shame, humiliation, and deep insult his aggrandizement so often involved were never deceived. We looked at
him clearly, with world-old eyes, and saw simply a human
thing, weak and pitiable and cruel, even as we are and were.

These super-men and world-mastering demi-gods listened, however, to no low tongues of ours, even when we
pointed silently to their feet of clay. Perhaps we, as folk of
simpler soul and more primitive type, have been most struck
in the welter of recent years by the utter failure of white reli-

gion. We have curled our lips in something like contempt as we have witnessed glib apology and weary explanation. Nothing of the sort deceived us. A nation's religion is its life, and as such white Christianity is a miserable failure.

Nor would we be unfair in this criticism: We know that we, too, have failed, as you have, and have rejected many a Buddha, even as you have denied Christ; but we acknowledge our human frailty, while you, claiming superhumanity, scoff endlessly at our shortcomings.

The number of white individuals who are practising with even reasonable approximation the democracy and unselfishness of Jesus Christ is so small and unimportant as to be fit subject for jest in Sunday supplements and in *Punch, Life, Le Rire,* and *Fliegende Blätter.* In her foreign mission work the extraordinary self-deception of white religion is epitomized: solemnly the white world sends five million dollars worth of missionary propaganda to Africa each year and in the same twelve months adds twenty-five million dollars worth of the vilest gin manufactured. Peace to the augurs of Rome!

We may, however, grant without argument that religious ideals have always far outrun their very human devotees. Let us, then, turn to more mundane matters of honor and fairness. The world today is trade. The world has turned shopkeeper; history is economic history; living is earning a living. Is it necessary to ask how much of high emprise and honorable conduct has been found here? Something, to be sure. The establishment of world credit systems is built on splendid and realizable faith in fellowmen. But it is, after all, so low and elementary a step that sometimes it looks merely like honor among thieves, for the revelations of highway robbery and low cheating in the business world and in all its great modern centers have raised in the hearts of all true men in our day an exceeding great cry for revolution in our basic methods and conceptions of industry and commerce.

We do not, for a moment, forget the robbery of other times and races when trade was a most uncertain gamble; but was there not a certain honesty and frankness in the evil that argued a saner morality? There are more merchants today, surer deliveries, and wider well-being, but are there not, also, bigger thieves, deeper injustice, and more calloused selfishness in well-being? Be that as it may,—certainly the nicer sense of honor that has risen ever and again in groups of forward-thinking men has been curiously and broadly blunted. Consider our chiefest industry,—fighting. Laboriously the Middle Ages built its rules of fairness— equal armament, equal notice, equal conditions. What do we see today? Machine-guns against assegais; conquest sugared with religion; mutilation and rape masquerading as culture,—all this, with vast applause at the superiority of white over black soldiers!

War is horrible! This the dark world knows to its awful cost. But has it just become horrible, in these last days, when under essentially equal conditions, equal armament, and equal waste of wealth white men are fighting white men, with surgeons and nurses hovering near?

Think of the wars through which we have lived in the last decade: in German Africa, in British Nigeria, in French and Spanish Morocco, in China, in Persia, in the Balkans, in Tripoli, in Mexico, and in a dozen lesser places—were not these horrible, too? Mind you, there were for most of these wars no Red Cross funds.

Behold little Belgium and her pitiable plight, but has the world forgotten Congo? What Belgium now suffers is not half, not even a tenth, of what she has done to black Congo since Stanley's great dream of 1880. Down the dark forests of inmost Africa sailed this modern Sir Galahad, in the name of "the noble-minded men of several nations," to introduce commerce and civilization. What came of it? "Rubber and murder, slavery in its worst form," wrote Glave in 1895.

Harris declares that King Leopold's regime meant the death of twelve million natives, "but what we who were behind the scenes felt most keenly was the fact that the real catastrophe in the Congo was desolation and murder in the larger sense. The invasion of family life, the ruthless destruction of every social barrier, the shattering of every tribal law, the introduction of criminal practices which struck the chiefs of the people dumb with horror—in a word, a veritable avalanche of filth and immorality over-whelmed the Congo tribes."

Yet the fields of Belgium laughed, the cities were gay, art and science flourished; the groans that helped to nourish this civilization fell on deaf ears because the world round about was doing the same sort of thing elsewhere on its own account.

As we saw the dead dimly through rifts of battle-smoke and heard faintly the cursings and accusations of blood brothers, we darker men said: This is not Europe gone mad; this is not aberration nor insanity; this *is* Europe; this seeming Terrible is the real soul of white culture—back of all culture,—stripped and visible today. This is where the world has arrived,—these dark and awful depths and not the shining and ineffable heights of which it boasted. Here is whither the might and energy of modern humanity has really gone.

But may not the world cry back at us and ask: "What better thing have you to show? What have you done or would do better than this if you had today the world rule? Paint with all riot of hateful colors the thin skin of European culture,—is it not better than any culture that arose in Africa or Asia?"

It is. Of this there is no doubt and never has been; but why is it better? Is it better because Europeans are better, nobler, greater, and more gifted than other folk? It is not. Europe has never produced and never will in our day bring forth a single human soul who cannot be matched and over-matched in every line of human endeavor by Asia and Africa. Run the gamut, if you will, and let us have the Europeans who in sober truth over-match Nefertari, Mohammed, Rameses and Askia, Confucius, Buddha, and Jesus Christ. If we could scan the calendar of thousands of lesser men, in like comparison, the result would be the same; but we cannot do this because of the deliberately educated ignorance of white schools by which they remember Napoleon and forget Sonni Ali.

The greatness of Europe has lain in the width of the stage on which she has played her part, the strength of the foundations on which she has builded, and a natural, human ability no whit greater (if as great) than that of other days and races. In other words, the deeper reasons for the triumph of European civilization lie quite outside and beyond Europe,—back in the universal struggles of all mankind.

Why, then, is Europe great? Because of the foundations which the mighty past have furnished her to build upon: the iron trade of ancient, black Africa, the religion and empire-building of yellow Asia, the art and science of the "dago" Mediterranean shore, east, south, and west, as well as north. And where she has builded securely upon this great past and learned from it she has gone forward to greater and more splendid human triumph; but where she has ignored this past and forgotten and sneered at it, she has shown the cloven hoof of poor, crucified humanity,—she has played, like other empires gone, the world fool!

If, then, European triumphs in culture have been greater, so, too, may her failures have been greater. How great a failure and a failure in what does the World War betoken? Was it national jealousy of the sort of the seventeenth century? But Europe has done more to break down national barriers than any preceding culture. Was it fear of the balance of power in Europe? Hardly, save in the half-Asiatic problems of the Balkans. What, then, does Hauptmann mean when he says: "Our jealous enemies forged an iron ring about our breasts and we knew our breasts had to expand,—that we had to split asunder this ring or else we had to cease breathing. But Germany will not cease to breathe and so it came to pass that the iron ring was forced apart."

Whither is this expansion? What is that breath of life, thought to be so indispensable to a great European nation? Manifestly it is expansion overseas; it is colonial aggrandizement which explains, and alone adequately explains, the World War. How many of us today fully realize the current theory of colonial expansion, of the relation of Europe which is white, to the world which is black and brown and yellow? Bluntly put, that theory is this: It is the duty of white Europe to divide up the darker world and administer it for Europe's good.

This Europe has largely done. The European world is using black and brown men for all the uses which men know. Slowly but surely white culture is evolving the theory that "darkies" are born beasts of burden for white folk. It were silly to think otherwise, cries the cultured world, with stronger and shriller accord. The supporting arguments grow and twist themselves in the mouths of merchant, scientist, soldier, traveler, writer, and missionary: Darker peoples are dark in mind as well as in body; of dark, uncertain, and imperfect descent; of frailer, cheaper stuff; they are cowards in the face of mausers and maxims; they have no feelings, aspirations, and loves; they are fools, illogical idiots,— "half-devil and half-child."

Such as they are civilization must, naturally, raise them, but soberly and in limited ways. They are not simply dark white men. They are not "men" in the sense that Europeans are men. To the very limited extent of their shallow capacities lift them to be useful to whites, to raise cotton, gather rubber, fetch ivory, dig diamonds,—and let them be paid what men think they are worth—white men who know them to be well-nigh worthless.

Such degrading of men by men is as old as mankind and the invention of no one race or people. Ever have men striven to conceive of their victims as different from the victors, endlessly different, in soul and blood, strength and cunning, race and lineage. It has been left, however, to Europe and to modern days to discover the eternal world-wide mark of meanness,—color!

Such is the silent revolution that has gripped modern European culture in the later nineteenth and twentieth centuries. Its zenith came in Boxer times: White supremacy was all but world-wide, Africa was dead, India conquered, Japan isolated, and China prostrate, while white America whetted her sword for mongrel Mexico and mulatto South America, lynching her own Negroes the while. Temporary halt in this program was made by little Japan and the white world immediately sensed the peril of such "yellow" presumption! What sort of a world would this be if yellow men must be treated "white"? Immediately the eventual overthrow of Japan became a subject of deep thought and intrigue, from

St. Petersburg to San Francisco, from the Key of Heaven to the Little Brother of the Poor.

The using of men for the benefit of masters is no new invention of modern Europe. It is quite as old as the world. But Europe proposed to apply it on a scale and with an elaborateness of detail of which no former world ever dreamed. The imperial width of the thing,—the heaven-defying audacity—makes its modern newness.

The scheme of Europe was no sudden invention, but a way out of long-pressing difficulties. It is plain to modern white civilization that the subjection of the white working classes cannot much longer be maintained. Education, political power, and increased knowledge of the technique and meaning of the industrial process are destined to make a more and more equitable distribution of wealth in the near future. The day of the very rich is drawing to a close, so far as individual white nations are concerned. But there is a loophole. There is a chance for exploitation on an immense scale for inordinate profit, not simply to the very rich, but to the middle class and to the laborers. This chance lies in the exploitation of darker peoples. It is here that the golden hand beckons. Here are no labor unions or votes or questioning onlookers or inconvenient consciences. These men may be used down to the very bone, and shot and maimed in "punitive" expeditions when they revolt. In these dark lands "industrial development" may repeat in exaggerated form every horror of the industrial history of Europe, from slavery and rape to disease and maiming, with only one test of success,—dividends!

This theory of human culture and its aims has worked itself through warp and woof of our daily thought with a thoroughness that few realize. Everything great, good, efficient, fair, and honorable is "white"; everything mean, bad, blundering, cheating, and dishonorable is "yellow"; a bad taste is "brown"; and the devil is "black." The changes of this theme are continually rung in picture and story, in newspaper heading and moving-picture, in sermon and school book, until, of course, the King can do no wrong,—a White Man is always right and a Black Man has no rights which a white man is bound to respect.

There must come the necessary despisings and hatreds of these savage half-men, this unclean *canaille* of the world—these dogs of men. All through the world this gospel is preaching. It has its literature, it has its priests, it has its secret propaganda and above all—it pays!

There's the rub,—it pays. Rubber, ivory, and palm-oil; tea, coffee, and cocoa; bananas, oranges, and other fruit; cotton, gold, and copper—they, and a hundred other things which dark and sweating bodies hand up to the white world from their pits of slime, pay and pay well, but of all that the world gets the black world gets only the pittance that the white world throws it disdainfully.

Small wonder, then, that in the practical world of things-that-be there is jealousy and strife for the possession of the labor of dark millions, for the right to bleed and exploit the colonies of the world where this golden stream may be had, not always for the asking, but surely for the whipping and shooting. It was this competition for the labor of yellow, brown, and black folks that was the cause of the World War. Other causes have been glibly given and other contributing causes there doubtless were, but they were subsidiary and subordinate to this vast quest of the dark world's wealth and toil.

Colonies, we call them, these places where "niggers" are cheap and the earth is rich; they are those outlands where like a swarm of hungry locusts white masters may settle to be served as kings, wield the lash of slave-drivers, rape girls and wives, grow as rich as Croesus and send homeward a golden stream. They belt the earth, these places, but they cluster in the tropics, with its darkened peoples: in Hong Kong and Anam, in Borneo and Rhodesia, in Sierra Leone and Nigeria, in Panama and Havana—these are the El Dorados toward which the world powers stretch itching palms.

Germany, at last one and united and secure on land, looked across the seas and seeing England with sources of wealth insuring a luxury and power which Germany could not hope to rival by the slower processes of exploiting her own peasants and workingmen, especially with these workers half in revolt, immediately built her navy and entered into a desperate competition for possession of colonies of darker peoples. To South America, to China, to Africa, to Asia Minor, she turned like a hound quivering on the leash, impatient, suspicious, irritable, with blood-shot eyes and dripping fangs, ready for the awful word. England and France crouched watchfully over their bones, growling and wary, but gnawing industriously, while the blood of the dark world whetted their greedy appetites. In the background, shut out from the highway to the seven seas, sat Russia and Austria, snarling and snapping at each other and at the last Mediterranean gate to the El Dorado, where the Sick Man enjoyed bad health, and where millions of serfs in the Balkans, Russia, and Asia offered a feast to greed well-nigh as great as Africa.

The fateful day came. It had to come. The cause of war is preparation for war; and of all that Europe has done in a century there is nothing that has equaled in energy, thought, and time her preparation for wholesale murder. The only adequate cause of this preparation was conquest and conquest, not in Europe, but primarily among the darker peoples of Asia and Africa; conquest, not for assimilation and uplift, but for commerce and degradation. For this, and this mainly, did Europe gird herself at frightful cost for war.

The red day dawned when the tinder was lighted in the Balkans and Austro-Hungary seized a bit which brought her a step nearer to the world's highway; she seized one bit and poised herself for another. Then came that curious chorus of challenges, those leaping suspicions, raking all causes for distrust and rivalry and hatred, but saying little of the real and greatest cause.

Each nation felt its deep interests involved. But how? Not, surely, in the death of Ferdinand the Warlike; not, surely, in the old, half-forgotten *revanche* for Alsace-Lorraine; not even in the neutrality of Belgium. No! But in the possession of land overseas, in the right to colonies, the chance to levy endless tribute on the darker world,—on coolies in China, on starving peasants in India, on black savages in Africa, on dying South Sea Islanders, on Indians of the Amazon—all this and nothing more.

Even the broken reed on which we had rested high hopes of eternal peace,—the guild of the laborers—the front of that very important movement for human justice on which we had builded most, even this flew like a straw before the breath of king and kaiser. Indeed, the flying had been foreshadowed when in Germany and America "international" Socialists had all but read yellow and black men out of the kingdom of industrial justice. Subtly had they been bribed, but effectively: Were they not lordly whites and should they not share in the spoils of rape? High wages in the United States and England might be the skilfully manipulated result of slavery in Africa and of peonage in Asia.

With the dog-in-the-manger theory of trade, with the determination to reap inordinate profits and to exploit the weakest to the utmost there came a new imperialism,—the rage for one's own nation to own the earth or, at least, a large enough portion of it to insure as big profits as the next nation. Where sections could not be owned by one dominant nation there came a policy of "open door," but the "door" was open to "white people only." As to the darkest and weakest of peoples there was but one unanimity in Europe,—that which Herr Dernberg of the German Colonial Office called the agreement with England to maintain white "prestige" in Africa,—the doctrine of the divine right of white people to steal.

Thus the world market most wildly and desperately sought today is the market where labor is cheapest and most helpless and profit is most abundant. This labor is kept cheap and helpless because the white world despises "darkies." If one has the temerity to suggest that these workingmen may walk the way of white workingmen and climb by votes and self-assertion and education to the rank of men, he is howled out of court. They cannot do it and if they could, they shall not, for they are the enemies of the white race and the whites shall rule forever and forever and everywhere. Thus the hatred and despising of human beings from whom Europe wishes to extort her luxuries has led to such jealousy and bickering between European nations that they have fallen afoul of each other and have fought like crazed beasts. Such is the fruit of human hatred.

But what of the darker world that watches? Most men belong to this world. With Negro and Negroid, East Indian, Chinese, and Japanese they form two-thirds of the population of the world. A belief in humanity is a belief in colored men. If the uplift of mankind must be done by men, then the destinies of this world will rest ultimately in the hands of darker nations.

What, then, is this dark world thinking? It is thinking that as wild and awful as this shameful war was, *it is nothing to compare with that fight for freedom which black and brown and yellow men must and will make unless their oppression and humiliation and insult at the hands of the White World cease. The Dark World is going to submit to its present treatment just as long as it must and not one moment longer.*

Let me say this again and emphasize it and leave no room for mistaken meaning: The World War was primarily the jealous and avaricious struggle for the largest share in exploiting darker races. As such it is and must be but the prelude to the armed and indignant protest of these despised and raped peoples. Today Japan is hammering on the door of justice, China is raising her half-manacled hands to knock next, India is writhing for the freedom to knock, Egypt is sullenly muttering, the Negroes of South and West Africa, of the West Indies, and of the United States are just awakening to their shameful slavery. Is, then, this war the end of wars? Can it be the end, so long as sits enthroned, even in the souls of those who cry peace, the despising and robbing of darker peoples? If Europe hugs this delusion, then this is not the end of world war,—it is but the beginning!

We see Europe's greatest sin precisely where we found Africa's and Asia's,—in human hatred, the despising of men; with this difference, however: Europe has the awful lesson of the past before her, has the splendid results of widened areas of tolerance, sympathy, and love among men, and she faces a greater, an infinitely greater, world of men than any preceding civilization ever faced.

It is curious to see America, the United States, looking on herself, first, as a sort of natural peacemaker, then as a moral protagonist in this terrible time. No nation is less fitted for this rôle. For two or more centuries America has marched proudly in the van of human hatred,—making bonfires of human flesh and laughing at them hideously, and making the insulting of millions more than a matter of dislike,—rather a great religion, a world war-cry: Up white, down black; to your tents, O white folk, and world war with black and parti-colored mongrel beasts!

Instead of standing as a great example of the success of democracy and the possibility of human brotherhood America has taken her place as an awful example of its pitfalls and failures, so far as black and brown and yellow peoples are concerned. And this, too, in spite of the fact that there has been no actual failure; the Indian is not dying out, the Japanese and Chinese have not menaced the land, and the experiment of Negro suffrage has resulted in the uplift of twelve million people at a rate probably unparalleled in history. But what of this? America, Land of Democracy, wanted to believe in the failure of democracy so far as darker peoples were concerned. Absolutely without excuse she established a caste system, rushed into preparation for war, and conquered tropical colonies. She stands today shoulder to shoulder with Europe in Europe's worst sin against civilization. She aspires to sit among the great nations who arbitrate the fate of "lesser breeds without the law" and she is at times heartily ashamed even of the large number of "new" white people whom her democracy has admitted to place and power. Against this surging forward of Irish and German, of Russian Jew, Slav and "dago" her social bars have not availed, but against Negroes she can and does take her unflinching and immovable stand, backed by this new public policy of Europe. She trains her immigrants to this despising of "niggers" from the day of their landing, and they carry and send the news back to the submerged classes in the fatherlands.

All this I see and hear up in my tower, above the thunder of the seven seas. From my narrowed windows I stare into the night that looms beneath the cloud-swept stars. Eastward and westward storms are breaking,—great, ugly whirlwinds of hatred and blood and cruelty. I will not believe them inevitable. I will not believe that all that was must be, that all the shameful drama of the past must be done again today before the sunlight sweeps the silver seas.

If I cry amid this roar of elemental forces, must my cry be in vain, because it is but a cry,—a small and human cry amid Promethean gloom?

Back beyond the world and swept by these wild, white faces of the awful dead, why will this Soul of White Folk,—this modern Prometheus,—hang bound by his own binding, tethered by a fable of the past? I hear his mighty cry reverberating through the world, "I am white!" Well and good, O Prometheus, divine thief! Is not the world wide enough for two colors, for many little shinings of the sun? Why, then, devour your own vitals if I answer even as proudly, "I am black!"

The Riddle of the Sphinx

Dark daughter of the lotus leaves that watch the Southern
    Sea!
Wan spirit of a prisoned soul a-panting to be free!
    The muttered music of thy streams, the whisper of the
        deep,
    Have kissed each other in God's name and kissed a
        world to sleep.

The will of the world is a whistling wind, sweeping a
    cloud-swept sky,
And not from the East and not from the West knelled that
    soul-waking cry,
    But out of the South,—the sad, black South—it
        screamed from the top of the sky,
    Crying: "Awake, O ancient race!" Wailing, "O woman,
        arise!"
And crying and sighing and crying again as a voice in the
    midnight cries,—
But the burden of white men bore her back and the white
    world stifled her sighs.

The white world's vermin and filth:
    All the dirt of London,
    All the scum of New York;
    Valiant spoilers of women
    And conquerors of unarmed men;
    Shameless breeders of bastards,

Drunk with the greed of gold,
Baiting their blood-stained hooks
With cant for the souls of the simple;
Bearing the white man's burden
Of liquor and lust and lies!
Unthankful we wince in the East,
Unthankful we wail from the westward,
Unthankfully thankful, we curse,
In the unworn wastes of the wild:
      I hate them, Oh!
      I hate them well,
      I hate them, Christ!
      As I hate hell!
      If I were God,
      I'd sound their knell
      This day!
Who raised the fools to their glory,
But black men of Egypt and Ind,
Ethiopia's sons of the evening,
Indians and yellow Chinese,
Arabian children of morning,
And mongrels of Rome and Greece?
      Ah, well!
And they that raised the boasters
Shall drag them down again,—
Down with the theft of their thieving
And murder and mocking of men;
Down with their barter of women
And laying and lying of creeds;
Down with their cheating of childhood
And drunken orgies of war,—
      down
          down
               deep down,

Till the devil's strength be shorn,
Till some dim, darker David, a-hoeing of his corn,
And married maiden, mother of God,
Bid the black Christ be born!
Then shall our burden be manhood,
Be it yellow or black or white;
And poverty and justice and sorrow,
The humble and simple and strong
Shall sing with the sons of morning
And daughters of even-song:
Black mother of the iron hills that ward the blazing sea,
Wild spirit of a storm-swept soul, a-struggling to be
    free,
Where 'neath the bloody finger-marks thy riven
    bosom quakes,
Thicken the thunders of God's Voice and lo! a world
    awakes!

III | THE HANDS OF ETHIOPIA

"*Semper novi quid ex Africa*," cried the Roman pro-consul, and he voiced the verdict of forty centuries. Yet there are those who would write world history and leave out of account this most marvelous of continents. Particularly today most men assume that Africa is far afield from the center of our burning social problems and especially from our problem of world war.

Always Africa is giving us something new or some metempsychosis of a world-old thing. On its black bosom arose one of the earliest, if not the earliest, of self-protecting civilizations, which grew so mightily that it still furnishes superlatives to thinking and speaking men. Out of its darker and more remote forest fastnesses came, if we may credit many recent scientists, the first welding of iron, and we know that agriculture and trade flourished there when Europe was a wilderness.

Nearly every human empire that has arisen in the world, material and spiritual, has found some of its greatest crises on this continent of Africa, from Greece to Great Britain. As Mommsen says: "It was through Africa that

Christianity became the religion of the world." In Africa the last flood of Germanic invasions spent itself within hearing of the last gasp of Byzantium, and it was through Africa that Islam came to play its great rôle of conqueror and civilizer.

With the Renaissance and the widened world of modern thought Africa came no less suddenly with her new-old gift. Shakespeare's "Ancient Pistol" cries:

> A foutre for the world and worldlings base!
> I speak of Africa and golden joys!

He echoes a legend of gold from the days of Punt and Ophir to those of Ghana, the Gold Coast, and the Rand. This thought had sent the world's greed scurrying down the hot, mysterious coasts of Africa to the Good Hope of gain, until for the first time a real world-commerce was born, albeit it started as a commerce mainly in the bodies and souls of men.

The present problem of problems is nothing more than democracy beating itself helplessly against the color bar,— purling, seeping, seething, foaming to burst through, ever and again overwhelming the emerging masses of white men in its rolling backwaters and held back by those who dream of future kingdoms of greed built on black and brown and yellow slavery.

The indictment of Africa against Europe is grave. For four hundred years white Europe was the chief support of that trade in human beings which first and last robbed black Africa of a hundred million human beings, transformed the face of her social life, overthrew organized government, distorted ancient industry, and snuffed out the lights of cultural development. Today instead of removing laborers from

Africa to distant slavery, industry built on a new slavery approaches Africa to deprive the natives of their land, to force them to toil, and to reap all the profit for the white world.

It is scarcely necessary to remind the reader of the essential facts underlying these broad assertions. A recent law of the Union of South Africa assigns nearly two hundred and fifty million acres of the best of natives' land to a million and a half whites and leaves thirty-six million acres of swamp and marsh for four and a half-million blacks. In Rhodesia over ninety million acres have been practically confiscated. In the Belgian Congo all the land was declared the property of the state.

Slavery in all but name has been the foundation of the cocoa industry in St. Thome and St. Principe and in the mines of the Rand. Gin has been one of the greatest of European imports, having increased fifty percent in ten years and reaching a total of at least twenty-five million dollars a year today. Negroes of ability have been carefully gotten rid of, deposed from authority, kept out of positions of influence, and discredited in their people's eyes, while a caste of white overseers and governing officials has appeared everywhere.

Naturally, the picture is not all lurid. David Livingstone has had his successors and Europe has given Africa something of value in the beginning of education and industry. Yet the balance of iniquity is desperately large; but worse than that, it has aroused no world protest. A great Englishman, familiar with African problems for a generation, says frankly today: "There does not exist any real international conscience to which you can appeal."

Moreover, that treatment shows no certain signs of abatement. Today in England the Empire Resources Development Committee proposes to treat African colonies as "crown

estates" and by intensive scientific exploitation of both land
and labor to make these colonies pay the English national
debt after the war! German thinkers, knowing the tremendous demand for raw material which would follow the war,
had similar plans of exploitation. "It is the clear, common
sense of the African situation," says H. G. Wells, "that while
these precious regions of raw material remain divided up
between a number of competitive European imperialisms,
each resolutely set upon the exploitation of its 'possessions' to
its own advantage and the disadvantage of the others, there
can be no permanent peace in the world. It is impossible."

We, then, who fought the war against war; who in a hell
of blood and suffering held hardly our souls in leash by the
vision of a world organized for peace; who are looking for
industrial democracy and for the organization of Europe so as
to avoid incentives to war,—we, least of all, should be willing
to leave the backward world as the greatest temptation, not
only to wars based on international jealousies, but to the most
horrible of wars,—which arise from the revolt of the mad-
dened against those who hold them in common contempt.

Consider, my reader,—if you were today a man of some
education and knowledge, but born a Japanese or a Chi-
naman, an East Indian or a Negro, what would you do and
think? What would be in the present chaos your outlook
and plan for the future? Manifestly, you would want
freedom for your people,—freedom from insult, from segregation, from poverty, from physical slavery. If the attitude
of the European and American worlds is in the future going
to be based essentially upon the same policies as in the past,
then there is but one thing for the trained man of darker
blood to do and that is definitely and as openly as possible
to organize his world for war against Europe. He may have
to do it by secret, underground propaganda, as in Egypt and

India and eventually in the United States; or by open increase of armament, as in Japan; or by desperate efforts at modernization, as in China; but he must do it. He represents the vast majority of mankind. To surrender would be far worse than physical death. There is no way out unless the white world opens the door. Either the white world gives up such insult as its modern use of the adjective "yellow" indicates, or its connotation of "chink" and "nigger" implies; either it gives up the plan of color serfdom which its use of the other adjective "white" implies, as indicating everything decent and every part of the world worth living in,—or trouble is written in the stars!

It is, therefore, of singular importance after disquieting delay to see the real Pacifist appear. Both England and Germany have recently been basing their claims to parts of black Africa on the wishes and interests of the black inhabitants. Lloyd George has declared "the general principle of national self-determination applicable at least to German Africa," while Chancellor Hertling once welcomed a discussion "on the reconstruction of the world's colonial possessions."

The demand that an Africa for Africans shall replace the present barbarous scramble for exploitation by individual states comes from singularly different sources. Colored America demands that "the conquered German colonies should not be returned to Germany, neither should they be held by the Allies. Here is the opportunity for the establishment of a nation that may never recur. Thousands of colored men, sick of white arrogance and hypocrisy, see in this their race's only salvation."

Sir Harry H. Johnston recently said: "If we are to talk, as we do, sentimentally but justly about restoring the nationhood of Poland, about giving satisfaction to the separatist feeling in Ireland, and about what is to be done for

European nations who are oppressed, then we can hardly exclude from this feeling the countries of Africa."

Laborers, black laborers, on the Canal Zone write: "Out of this chaos may be the great awakening of our race. There is cause for rejoicing. If we fail to embrace this opportunity now, we fail to see how we will be ever able to solve the race question. It is for the British Negro, the French Negro, and the American Negro to rise to the occasion and start a national campaign, jointly and collectively, with this aim in view."

From British West Africa comes the bitter complaint "that the West Africans should have the right or opportunity to settle their future for themselves is a thing which hardly enters the mind of the European politician. That the Balkan States should be admitted to the Council of Peace and decide the government under which they are to live is taken as a matter of course because they are Europeans, but no extra-European is credited, even by the extremest advocates of human equality, with any right except to humbly accept the fate which Europe shall decide for him."

Here, then, is the danger and the demand; and the real Pacifist will seek to organize, not simply the masses in white nations, guarding against exploitation and profiteering, but will remember that no permanent relief can come but by including in this organization the lowest and the most exploited races in the world. World philanthropy, like national philanthropy, must come as uplift and prevention and not merely as alleviation and religious conversion. Reverence for humanity, as such, must be installed in the world, and Africa should be the talisman.

Black Africa, including British, French, Belgian, Portuguese, Italian, and Spanish possessions and the independent states of Abyssinia and Liberia and leaving out of account Egypt and North Africa, on the one hand, and South Africa, on the other, has an area of 8,200,000 square miles and a population well over one hundred millions of black men, with less than one hundred thousand whites.

Commercial exploitation in Africa has already larger results to show than most people realize. Annually $200,000,000 worth of goods was coming out of black Africa before the World War, including a third of the world's supply of rubber, a quarter of all of the world's cocoa, and practically all of the world's cloves, gum-arabic, and palm-oil. In exchange there was being returned to Africa one hundred millions in cotton cloth, twenty-five millions in iron and steel, and as much in foods, and probably twenty-five millions in liquors.

Here are the beginnings of a modern industrial system: iron and steel for permanent investment, bound to yield large dividends; cloth as the cheapest exchange for invaluable raw material; liquor to tickle the appetites of the natives and render the alienation of land and the break-down of customary law easier; eventually forced and contract labor under white drivers to increase and systematize the production of raw materials. These materials are capable of indefinite expansion: cotton may yet challenge the southern United States, fruits and vegetables, hides and skins, lumber and dye-stuffs, coffee and tea, grain and tobacco, and fibers of all sorts can easily follow organized and systematic toil.

Is it a paradise of industry we thus contemplate? It is much more likely to be a hell. Under present plans there will be no voice or law or custom to protect labor, no trades unions, no eight-hour laws, no factory legislation,—nothing of that great body of legislation built up in modern days to protect mankind from sinking to the level of beasts of burden. All the industrial deviltry, which civilization has

been driving to the slums and the backwaters, will have a
voiceless continent to conceal it. If the slave cannot be
taken from Africa, slavery can be taken to Africa.

Who are the folk who live here? They are brown and
black, curly and crisp-haired, short and tall, and long-
headed. Out of them in days without date flowed the
beginnings of Egypt; among them rose, later, centers of culture at Ghana, Melle, and Timbuktu. Kingdoms and
empires flourished in Songhay and Zymbabwe, and art and
industry in Yoruba and Benin. They have fought every
human calamity in its most hideous form and yet today they
hold some similar vestiges of a mighty past,—their work in
iron, their weaving and carving, their music and singing,
their tribal government, their town-meeting and market-
place, their desperate valor in war.

Missionaries and commerce have left some good with
all their evil. In black Africa today there are more than a
thousand government schools and some thirty thousand
mission schools, with a more or less regular attendance of
three-quarters of a million school children. In a few cases
training of a higher order is given chiefs' sons and selected
pupils. These beginnings of education are not much for so
vast a land and there is no general standard or set plan of
development, but, after all, the children of Africa are beginning to learn.

In black Africa today only one-seventeenth of the land
and a ninth of the people in Liberia and Abyssinia are
approximately independent, although menaced and policed
by European capitalism. Half the land and the people are in
domains under Portugal, France, and Belgium, held with
the avowed idea of exploitation for the benefit of Europe
under a system of caste and color serfdom. Out of this dangerous nadir of development stretch two paths: one is indi-

cated by the condition of about three percent of the people who in Sierra Leone, the Gold Coast, and French Senegal, are tending toward the path of modern development; the other path, followed by a fourth of the land and people, has local self-government and native customs and might evolve, if undisturbed, a native culture along their own peculiar lines. A tenth of the land, sparsely settled, is being monopolized and held for whites to make an African Australia. To these later folk must be added the four and one-half millions of the South African Union, who by every modern device are being forced into landless serfdom.

Before the World War tendencies were strongly toward the destruction of independent Africa, the industrial slavery of the mass of the blacks and the encouragement of white immigration, where possible, to hold the blacks in subjection.

Against this idea let us set the conception of a new African World State, a Black Africa, applying to these peoples the splendid pronouncements which have of late been so broadly and perhaps carelessly given the world: recognizing in Africa the declaration of the American Federation of Labor, that "no people must be forced under sovereignty under which it does not wish to live"; recognizing in President Wilson's message to the Russians, the "principle of the undictated development of all peoples"; recognizing the resolution of the recent conference of the Aborigines Protection Society of England, "that in any reconstruction of Africa, which may result from this war, the interests of the native inhabitants and also their wishes, in so far as those wishes can be clearly ascertained, should be recognized as among the principal factors upon which the decision of their destiny should be based." In other words, recognizing for the first time in the history of the modern world that black men are human.

It may not be possible to build this state at once. With the victory of the Entente Allies, the German colonies, with their million of square miles and one-half million black inhabitants, should form such a nucleus. It would give Black Africa its physical beginnings. Beginning with the German colonies two other sets of colonies could be added, for obvious reasons. Neither Portugal nor Belgium has shown any particular capacity for governing colonial peoples. Valid excuses may in both cases be advanced, but it would certainly be fair to Belgium to have her start her great task of reorganization after the World War with neither the burden nor the temptation of colonies; and in the same way Portugal has, in reality, the alternative of either giving up her colonies to an African State or to some other European State in the near future. These two sets of colonies would add 1,700,000 square miles and eighteen million inhabitants. It would not, however, be fair to despoil Germany, Belgium, and Portugal of their colonies unless, as Count Hertling once demanded, the whole question of colonies be opened.

How far shall the modern world recognize nations which are not nations, but combinations of a dominant caste and a suppressed horde of serfs? Will it not be possible to rebuild a world with compact nations, empires of self-governing elements, and colonies of backward peoples under benevolent international control?

The great test would be easy. Does England propose to erect in India and Nigeria nations brown and black which shall be eventually independent, self-governing entities, with a full voice in the British Imperial Government? If not, let these states either have independence at once or, if unfitted for that, be put under international tutelage and guardianship. It is possible that France, with her great heart, may welcome a Black France,—an enlarged Senegal in Africa; but it would seem that eventually all Africa south of twenty degrees north latitude and north of the Union of South Africa should be included in a new African State. Somaliland and Eritrea should be given to Abyssinia, and then with Liberia we would start with two small, independent African states and one large state under international control.

Does this sound like an impossible dream? No one could be blamed for so regarding it before 1914. I, myself, would have agreed with them. But since the nightmare of 1914-1918, since we have seen the impossible happen and the unspeakable become so common as to cease to stir us; in a day when Russia has dethroned her Czar, England has granted the suffrage to women and is in the act of giving Home Rule to Ireland; when Germany has adopted parliamentary government; when Jerusalem has been delivered from the Turks; and the United States has taken control of its railroads,—is it really so far-fetched to think of an Africa for the Africans, guided by organized civilization?

No one would expect this new state to be independent and self-governing from the start. Contrary, however, to present schemes for Africa the world would expect independence and self-government as the only possible end of the experiment. At first we can conceive of no better way of governing this state than through that same international control by which we hope to govern the world for peace. A curious and instructive parallel has been drawn by Simeon Strunsky: "Just as the common ownership of the northwest territory helped to weld the colonies into the United States, so could not joint and benevolent domination of Africa and of other backward parts of the world be a cornerstone upon which the future federation of the world could be built?"

From the British Labor Party comes this declaration:

"With regard to the colonies of the several belligerents in tropical Africa, from sea to sea, the British Labor Movement disclaims all sympathy with the imperialist idea that these should form the booty of any nation, should be exploited for the profit of the capitalists, or should be used for the promotion of the militarists' aims of government. In view of the fact that it is impracticable here to leave the various peoples concerned to settle their own destinies it is suggested that the interests of humanity would be best served by the full and frank abandonment by all the belligerents of any dreams of an African Empire; the transfer of the present colonies of the European Powers in tropical Africa, however, and the limits of this area may be defined to the proposed Supernational Authority, or League of Nations."

Lloyd George himself has said in regard to the German colonies a word difficult to restrict merely to them: "I have repeatedly declared that they are held at the disposal of a conference, whose decision must have primary regard to the wishes and interests of the native inhabitants of such colonies. None of those territories is inhabited by Europeans. The governing consideration, therefore, must be that the inhabitants should be placed under the control of an administration acceptable to themselves, one of whose main purposes will be to prevent their exploitation for the benefit of European capitalists or governments."

The special commission for the government of this African State must, naturally, be chosen with great care and thought. It must represent, not simply governments, but civilization, science, commerce, social reform, religious philanthropy without sectarian propaganda. It must include, not simply white men, but educated and trained men of Negro blood. The guiding principles before such a commission should be clearly understood. In the first place, it ought by this time to be realized by the labor movement throughout the world that no industrial democracy can be built on industrial despotism, whether the two systems are in the same country or in different countries, since the world today so nearly approaches a common industrial unity. If, therefore, it is impossible in any single land to uplift permanently skilled labor without also raising common labor, so, too, there can be no permanent uplift of American or European labor as long as African laborers are slaves.

Secondly, this building of a new African State does not mean the segregation in it of all the world's black folk. It is too late in the history of the world to go back to the idea of absolute racial segregation. The new African State would not involve any idea of a vast transplantation of the twenty-seven million Negroids of the western world, of Africa, or of the gathering there of Negroid Asia. The Negroes in the United States and the other Americas have earned the right to fight out their problems where they are, but they could easily furnish from time to time technical experts, leaders of thought, and missionaries of culture for their backward brethren in the new Africa.

With these two principles, the practical policies to be followed out in the government of the new states should involve a thorough and complete system of modern education, built upon the present government, religion, and customary laws of the natives. There should be no violent tampering with the curiously efficient African institutions of local self-government through the family and the tribe; there should be no attempt at sudden "conversion" by religious propaganda. Obviously deleterious customs and unsanitary usages must gradually be abolished, but the general government, set up from without, must follow the example of the best colonial administrators and build on recognized, established foundations rather than from entirely new and theoretical plans.

The real effort to modernize Africa should be through schools rather than churches. Within ten years, twenty million black children ought to be in school. Within a generation young Africa should know the essential outlines of modern culture and groups of bright African students could be going to the world's great universities. From the beginning the actual general government should use both colored and white officials and later natives should be worked in. Taxation and industry could follow the newer ideals of industrial democracy, avoiding private land monopoly and poverty, and promoting co-operation in production and the socialization of income. Difficulties as to capital and revenue would be far less than many imagine. If a capable English administrator of British Nigeria could with $1,500 build up a cocoa industry of twenty million dollars annually, what might not be done in all Africa, without gin, thieves, and hypocrisy?

Capital could not only be accumulated in Africa, but attracted from the white world, with one great difference from present usage: no return so fabulous would be offered that civilized lands would be tempted to divert to colonial trade and invest materials and labor needed by the masses at home, but rather would receive the same modest profits as legitimate home industry offers.

There is no sense in asserting that the ideal of an African State, thus governed and directed toward independence and self-government, is impossible of realization. The first great essential is that the civilized world believe in its possibility. By reason of a crime (perhaps the greatest crime in human history) the modern world has been systematically taught to despise colored peoples. Men of edu-

cation and decency ask, and ask seriously, if it is really possible to uplift Africa. Are Negroes human, or, if human,
developed far enough to absorb, even under benevolent
tutelage, any appreciable part of modern culture? Has not
the experiment been tried in Haiti and Liberia, and failed?

One cannot ignore the extraordinary fact that a world
campaign beginning with the slave-trade and ending with
the refusal to capitalize the word "Negro," leading through
a passionate defense of slavery by attributing every bestiality
to blacks and finally culminating in the evident modern
profit which lies in degrading blacks,—all this has unconsciously trained millions of honest, modern men into the
belief that black folk are sub-human. This belief is not
based on science, else it would be held as a postulate of the
most tentative kind, ready at any time to be withdrawn in
the face of facts; the belief is not based on history, for it is
absolutely contradicted by Egyptian, Greek, Roman,
Byzantine, and Arabian experience; nor is the belief based
on any careful survey of the social development of men of
Negro blood to-day in Africa and America. It is simply passionate, deep-seated heritage, and as such can be moved by
neither argument nor fact. Only faith in humanity will lead
the world to rise above its present color prejudice.

Those who do believe in men, who know what black
men have done in human history, who have taken pains to
follow even superficially the story of the rise of the Negro in
Africa, the West Indies, and the Americas of our day know
that our modern contempt of Negroes rests upon no scientific foundation worth a moment's attention. It is nothing
more than a vicious habit of mind. It could as easily be over-
thrown as our belief in war, as our international hatreds, as
our old conception of the status of women, as our fear of
educating the masses, and as our belief in the necessity of

poverty. We can, if we will, inaugurate on the Dark Continent a last great crusade for humanity. With Africa redeemed Asia would be safe and Europe indeed triumphant.

I have not mentioned North and South Africa, because my eye was centered on the main mass of the Negro race. Yet it is clear that for the development of Central Africa, Egypt should be free and independent, there along the highway to a free and independent India; while Morocco, Algeria, Tunis, and Tripoli must become a part of Europe, with modern development and home rule. South Africa, stripped of its black serfs and their lands, must admit the resident natives and colored folk to its body politic as equals.

The hands which Ethiopia shall soon stretch out unto God are not mere hands of helplessness and supplication, but rather are they hands of pain and promise; hard, gnarled, and muscled for the world's real work; they are hands of fellowship for the half-submerged masses of a distempered world; they are hands of helpfulness for an agonized God!

Twenty centuries before Christ a great cloud swept over seas and settled on Africa, darkening and well-nigh blotting out the culture of the land of Egypt. For half a thousand years it rested there, until a black woman, Queen Nefertari, "the most venerated figure in Egyptian history," rose to the throne of the Pharaohs and redeemed the world and her people. Twenty centuries after Christ, Black Africa,—prostrated, raped, and shamed, lies at the feet of the conquering Philistines of Europe. Beyond the awful sea a black woman is weeping and waiting, with her sons on her breast. What shall the end be? The world-old and fearful things,—war and wealth, murder and luxury? Or shall it be a new thing,—a new peace and a new democracy of all races,—a great humanity of equal men? *"Semper novi quid ex Africa!"*

The Princess of the Hither Isles

Her soul was beautiful, wherefore she kept it veiled in lightly-laced humility and fear, out of which peered anxiously and anon the white and blue and pale-gold of her face,—beautiful as daybreak or as the laughing of a child. She sat in the Hither Isles, well walled between the This and Now, upon a low and silver throne, and leaned upon its armposts, sadly looking upward toward the sun. Now the Hither Isles are flat and cold and swampy, with drear-drab light and all manner of slimy, creeping things, and piles of dirt and clouds of flying dust and sordid scraping and feeding and noise.

She hated them and ever as her hands and busy feet swept back the dust and slime her soul sat silver-throned, staring toward the great hill to the westward, which shone so brilliant-golden beneath the sunlight and above the sea.

The sea moaned and with it moaned the princess' soul, for she was lonely,—very, very lonely, and full weary of the monotone of life. So she was glad to see a moving in Yonder Kingdom on the mountainside, where the sun shone warm, and when the king of Yonder Kingdom, silken in robe and golden-crowned and warded by his hound, walked down along the restless waters and sat beside the armpost of her throne, she wondered why she could not love him and fly with him up the shining mountain's side, out of the dirt and dust that nested between the This and Now. She looked at him and tried to be glad, for he was bonny and good to look upon, this king of Yonder Kingdom,—tall and straight, thin-lipped and white and tawny. So, again, this last day, she strove to burn life into his singularly sodden clay,—to put his icy soul aflame wherewith to warm her own, to set his senses singing. Vacantly he heard her winged words, staring and curling his long mustaches with vast thoughtfulness. Then he said:

"We've found more gold in Yonder Kingdom."

"Hell seize your gold!" blurted the princess.

"No,—it's mine," he maintained stolidly.

She raised her eyes. "It belongs," she said, "to the Empire of the Sun."

"Nay,—the Sun belongs to us," said the king calmly as he glanced to where Yonder Kingdom blushed above the sea. She glanced, too, and a softness crept into her eyes.

"No, no," she murmured as with hesitating pause she raised her eyes above the sea, above the hill, up into the sky where the sun hung silent and splendid. Its robes were heaven's blue, lined and broidered in living flame, and its crown was one vast jewel, glistening in glittering glory that made the sun's own face a blackness,—the blackness of utter light. With blinded, tear-filled eyes she peered into that formless black and burning face and sensed in its soft, sad gleam unfathomed understanding. With sudden, wild abandon she stretched her arms toward it appealing, beseeching, entreating, and lo!

"Niggers and dagoes," said the king of Yonder Kingdom, glancing carelessly backward and lighting in his lips a carefully rolled wisp of fragrant tobacco. She looked back, too, but in half-wondering terror, for it seemed—

A beggar man was creeping across the swamp, shuffling through the dirt and slime. He was little and bald and black, rough-clothed, sodden with dirt, and bent with toil. Yet withal something she sensed about him and it seemed,—

The king of Yonder Kingdom lounged more comfortably beside the silver throne and let curl a tiny trail of light-blue smoke.

"I hate beggars," he said, "especially brown and black ones." And he then pointed at the beggar's retinue and laughed,—an unpleasant laugh, welded of contempt and amusement. The princess looked and shrank on her throne. He, the beggar man, was—was what? But his retinue,—that squalid, sordid, parti-colored band of vacant, dull-faced filth and viciousness—was writhing over the land, and he and they seemed almost crouching underneath the scorpion lash of one tall skeleton, that looked like Death, and the twisted woman whom men called Pain. Yet they all walked as one.

The king of Yonder Kingdom laughed, but the princess shrank on her throne, and the king on seeing her thus took a gold-piece from out of his purse and tossed it carelessly to the passing throng. She watched it with fascinated eyes,—how it rose and sailed and whirled and struggled in the air, then seemed to burst, and upward flew its light and sheen and downward dropped its dross. She glanced at the king, but he was lighting a match. She watched the dross wallow in the slime, but the sunlight fell on the back of the beggar's neck, and he turned his head.

The beggar passing afar turned his head and the princess straightened on her throne; he turned his head and she shivered forward on her silver seat; he looked upon her full and slow and suddenly she saw within that formless black and burning face the same soft, glad gleam of utter understanding, seen so many times before. She saw the suffering of endless years and endless love that softened it. She saw the burning passion of the sun and with it the cold, unbending duty-deeds of upper air. All she had seen and dreamed of seeing in the rising, blazing sun she saw now again and with it myriads more of human tenderness, of longing, and of love. So, then, she knew. She rose as to a dream come true, with solemn face and waiting eyes.

With her rose the king of Yonder Kingdom, almost eagerly.

"You'll come?" he cried. "You'll come and see my gold?" And then in sudden generosity, he added: "You'll have a golden throne,—up there—when we marry."

But she, looking up and on with radiant face, answered softly: "I come."

So down and up and on they mounted,—the black beggar man and his cavalcade of Death and Pain, and then a space; and then a lone, black hound that nosed and whimpered as he ran, and then a space; and then the king of Yonder Kingdom in his robes, and then a space; and last the princess of the Hither Isles, with face set sunward and love-light in her eyes.

And so they marched and struggled on and up through endless years and spaces and ever the black beggar looked back past death and pain toward the maid and ever the maid strove forward with lovelit eyes, but ever the great and silken shoulders of the king of Yonder Kingdom arose between the princess and the sun like a cloud of storms.

Now, finally, they neared unto the hillside's topmost shoulder and there most eagerly the king bent to the bowels of the earth and bared its golden entrails,—all green and gray and rusted—while the princess strained her pitiful eyes aloft to where the beggar, set 'twixt Death and Pain, whirled his slim back against the glory of the setting sun and stood somber in his grave majesty, enhaloed and transfigured, out-stretching his long arms, and around all heaven glittered jewels in a cloth of gold.

A while the princess stood and moaned in mad amaze,

then with one wilful wrench she bared the white flowers of her breast and snatching forth her own red heart held it with one hand aloft while with the other she gathered close her robe and poised herself.

The king of Yonder Kingdom looked upward quickly, curiously, still fingering the earth, and saw the offer of her bleeding heart.

"It's a Negro!" he growled darkly; "it may not be."

The woman quivered.

"It's a nigger!" he repeated fiercely. "It's neither God nor man, but a nigger!"

The princess stepped forward.

The king grasped his sword and looked north and east; he raised his sword and looked south and west.

"I seek the sun," the princess sang, and started into the west.

"Never!" cried the king of Yonder Kingdom, "for such were blasphemy and defilement and the making of all evil."

So, raising his great sword he struck with all his might, and more. Down hissed the blow and it bit that little, white, heart-holding hand until it flew armless and disbodied up through the sunlit air. Down hissed the blow and it clove the whimpering hound until his last shriek shook the stars. Down hissed the blow and it rent the earth. It trembled, fell apart, and yawned to a chasm wide as earth from heaven, deep as hell, and empty, cold, and silent.

On yonder distant shore blazed the mighty Empire of the Sun in warm and blissful radiance, while on this side, in shadows cold and dark, gloomed the Hither Isles and the hill that once was golden, but now was green and slimy dross; all below was the sad and moaning sea, while between the Here and There flew the severed hand and dripped the bleeding heart.

Then up from the soul of the princess welled a cry of dark despair,—such a cry as only babe-raped mothers know and murdered loves. Poised on the crumbling edge of that great nothingness the princess hung, hungering with her eyes and straining her fainting ears against the awful splendor of the sky.

Out from the slime and shadows groped the king, thundering: "Back—don't be a fool!"

But down through the thin ether thrilled the still and throbbing warmth of heaven's sun, whispering "Leap!"

And the princess leapt.

IV | OF WORK AND WEALTH

For fifteen years I was a teacher of youth. They were years out of the fullness and bloom of my younger manhood. They were years mingled of half breathless work, of anxious self-questionings, of planning and replanning, of disillusion, or mounting wonder.

The teacher's life is a double one. He stands in a certain fear. He tends to be stilted, almost dishonest, veiling himself before those awful eyes. Not the eyes of Almighty God are so straight, so penetrating, so all-seeing as the wonder-swept eyes of youth. You walk into a room: to the left is a tall window, bright with colors of crimson and gold and sunshine. Here are rows of books and there is a table. Somber blackboards clothe the walls to the right and beside your desk is the delicate ivory of a nobly cast head. But you see nothing of this: you see only a silence and eyes,—fringed, soft eyes; hard eyes; eyes great and small; eyes here so poignant with beauty that the sob struggles in your throat; eyes there so hard with sorrow that laughter wells up to meet and beat it back; eyes through which the mockery and ridicule of hell or some pulse of high heaven may suddenly flash. Ah! That mighty pause before the class,—that orison and benediction—how much of my life it has been and made.

I fought earnestly against posing before my class. I tried to be natural and honest and frank, but it was bitter hard. What would you say to a soft, brown face, aureoled in a thousand ripples of gray-black hair, which knells suddenly: "Do you trust white people?" You do not and you know that you do not, much as you want to; yet you rise and lie and say you do; you must say it for her salvation and the world's; you repeat that she must trust them, that most white folks are honest, and all the while you are lying and every level, silent eye there knows you are lying, and miserably you sit and lie on, to the greater glory of God.

I taught history and economics and something called "sociology" at Atlanta University, where, as our Mr. Webster used to say, we professors occupied settees and not mere chairs. I was fortunate with this teaching in having vivid in the minds of my pupils a concrete social problem of which we all were parts and which we desperately desired to solve. There was little danger, then, of my teaching or of their thinking becoming purely theoretical. Work and wage were thrilling realities to us all. What did we study? I can tell you best by taking a concrete human case, such as was continually leaping to our eyes and thought and demanding understanding and interpretation and what I could bring of prophecy.

St. Louis sprawls where mighty rivers meet,—as broad as Philadelphia, but three stories high instead of two, with wider streets and dirtier atmosphere, over the dull-brown of wide, calm rivers. The city overflows into the valleys of Illinois and lies there, writhing under its grimy cloud. The other city is dusty and hot beyond all dream,—a feverish Pittsburg in the Mississippi Valley—a great, ruthless, terrible thing! It is the sort that crushes man and invokes some living

super-man,—a giant of things done, a clang of awful
accomplishment.

Three men came wandering across this place. They were
neither kings nor wise men, but they came with every significance—perhaps even greater—than that which the kings
bore in the days of old. There was one who came from the
North,—brawny and riotous with energy, a man of concen-
trated power, who held all the thunderbolts of modern capital in his great fists and made flour and meat, iron and steel,
cunning chemicals, wood, paint and paper, transforming to
endless tools a disemboweled earth. He was one who saw
nothing, knew nothing, sought nothing but the making and
buying of that which sells; who out from the magic of his
hand rolled over miles of iron road, ton upon ton of food
and metal and wood, of coal and oil and lumber, until the
thronging of knotted ways in East and real St. Louis was like
the red, festering ganglia of some mighty heart.

Then from the East and called by the crash of thunderbolts and forked-flame came the Unwise Man,—unwise by
the theft of endless ages, but as human as anything God ever
made. He was the slave for the miracle maker. It was he that
the thunderbolts struck and electrified into gasping energy.
The rasp of his hard breathing shook the midnights of all
this endless valley and the pulse of his powerful arms set the
great nation to trembling.

And then, at last, out of the South, like a still, small
voice, came the third man,—black, with great eyes and
greater memories; hesitantly eager and yet with the infinite
softness and ancient calm which come from that eternal race
whose history is not the history of a day, but of endless ages.
Here, surely, was fit meeting-place for these curiously intent
forces, for these epoch-making and age-twisting forces, for
these human feet on their super-human errands.

Yesterday I rode in East St. Louis. It is the kind of place one quickly recognizes,—tireless and with no restful green of verdure; hard and uneven of street; crude, cold, and even hateful of aspect; conventional, of course, in its business quarter, but quickly beyond one sees the ruts and the hollows, the stench of ill-tamed sewerage, unguarded railroad crossings, saloons outnumbering churches and churches catering to saloons; homes impudently strait and new, prostitutes free and happy, gamblers in paradise, the town "wide open," shameless and frank; great factories pouring out stench, filth, and flame—these and all other things so familiar in the world market places, where industry triumphs over thought and products overwhelm men. May I tell, too, how yesterday I rode in this city past flame-swept walls and over gray ashes; in streets almost wet with blood and beside ruins, where the bones of dead men newbleached peered out at me in sullen wonder?

Across the river, in the greater city, where bronze St. Louis,—that just and austere king—looks with angry, fearswept eyes down from the rolling heights of Forest Park, which knows him not nor heeds him, there is something of the same thing, but this city is larger and older and the forces of evil have had some curbing from those who have seen the vision and panted for life; but eastward from St. Louis there is a land of no taxes for great industries; there is a land where you may buy grafting politicians at far less rate than you would pay for franchises or privileges in a modern town. There, too, you may escape the buying of indulgences from the great terminal fist, which squeezes industry out of St. Louis. In fact, East St. Louis is a paradise for high and frequent dividends and for the piling up of wealth to be spent in St. Louis and Chicago and New York and when the world is sane again, across the seas.

So the Unwise Men pouring out of the East,—falling, scrambling, rushing into America at the rate of a million a year,—ran, walked, and crawled to this maelstrom of the workers. They garnered higher wage than ever they had before, but not all of it came in cash. A part, and an insidious part, was given to them transmuted into whiskey, prostitutes, and games of chance. They laughed and disported themselves. God! Had not their mothers wept enough? It was a good town. There was no veil of hypocrisy here, but a wickedness, frank, ungilded, and open. To be sure, there were things sometimes to reveal the basic savagery and thin veneer. Once, for instance, a man was lynched for brawling on the public square of the county seat; once a mayor who sought to "clean up" was publicly assassinated; always there was theft and rumors of theft, until St. Clair County was a hissing in good men's ears; but always, too, there were good wages and jolly hoodlums and unchecked wassail of Saturday nights. Gamblers, big and little, rioted in East St. Louis. The little gamblers used cards and roulette wheels and filched the weekly wage of the workers. The greater gamblers used meat and iron and undid the foundations of the world. All the gods of chance flaunted their wild raiment here, above the brown flood of the Mississippi.

Then the world changed; then civilization, built for culture, rebuilt itself for wilful murder in Europe, Asia, America, and the Southern Seas. Hands that made food made powder, and iron for railways was iron for guns. The wants of common men were forgotten before the groan of giants. Streams of gold, lost from the world's workers, filtered and trickled into the hands of gamblers and put new power into the thunderbolts of East St. Louis.

Wages had been growing before the World War. Slowly but remorselessly the skilled and intelligent, banding themselves, had threatened the coffers of the mighty, and slowly the mighty had disgorged. Even the common workers, the poor and unlettered, had again and again gripped the sills of the city walls and pulled themselves to their chins; but, alas! there were so many hands and so many mouths and the feet of the Disinherited kept coming across the wet paths of the sea to this old El Dorado.

War brought subtle changes. Wages stood still while prices fattened. It was not that the white American worker was threatened with starvation, but it was what was, after all, a more important question,—whether or not he should lose his front-room and victrola and even the dream of a Ford car.

There came a whirling and scrambling among the workers,—they fought each other; they climbed on each others' backs. The skilled and intelligent, banding themselves even better than before, bargained with the men of might and held them by bitter threats; the less skilled and more ignorant seethed at the bottom and tried, as of old, to bring it about that the ignorant and unlettered should learn to stand together against both capital and skilled labor.

It was here that there came out of the East a beam of unearthly light,—a triumph of possible good in evil so strange that the workers hardly believed it. Slowly they saw the gates of Ellis Island closing, slowly the footsteps of the yearly million men became fainter and fainter, until the stream of immigrants overseas was stopped by the shadow of death at the very time when new murder opened new markets over all the world to American industry; and the giants with the thunderbolts stamped and raged and peered out across the world and called for men and evermore,—men!

The Unwise Men laughed and squeezed reluctant dollars out of the fists of the mighty and saw in their dream the vision of a day when labor, as they knew it, should come into its own; saw this day and saw it with justice and with right, save for one thing, and that was the sound of the moan of the Disinherited, who still lay without the walls. When they heard this moan and saw that it came not across the seas, they were at first amazed and said it was not true; and then they were mad and said it should not be. Quickly they turned and looked into the red blackness of the South and in their hearts were fear and hate!

What did they see? They saw something at which they had been taught to laugh and make sport; they saw that which the heading of every newspaper column, the lie of every cub reporter, the exaggeration of every press dispatch, and the distortion of every speech and book had taught them was a mass of despicable men, inhuman; at best, laughable; at worst, the meat of mobs and fury.

What did they see? They saw nine and one-half millions of human beings. They saw the spawn of slavery, ignorant by law and by deviltry, crushed by insult and debauched by systematic and criminal injustice. They saw a people whose helpless women have been raped by thousands and whose men lynched by hundreds in the face of a sneering world. They saw a people with heads bloody, but unbowed, working faithfully at wages fifty percent lower than the wages of the nation and under conditions which shame civilization, saving homes, training children, hoping against hope. They saw the greatest industrial miracle of modern days,—slaves transforming themselves to freemen and climbing out of perdition by their own efforts, despite the most contemptible opposition God ever saw,—they saw all this and what they saw the distraught employers of America saw, too.

The North called to the South. A scream of rage went up from the cotton monopolists and industrial barons of the new South. Who was this who dared to "interfere" with their labor? Who sought to own their black slaves but they? Who honored and loved "niggers" as they did?

They mobilized all the machinery of modern oppression: taxes, city ordinances, licenses, state laws, municipal regulations, wholesale police arrests and, of course, the peculiarly Southern method of the mob and the lyncher. They appealed franctically to the United States Government; they groveled on their knees and shed wild tears at the "suffering" of their poor, misguided black friends, and yet, despite this, the Northern employers simply had to offer two and three dollars a day and from one-quarter to one-half a million dark workers arose and poured themselves into the North. They went to the mines of West Virginia, because war needs coal; they went to the industries of New Jersey and Pennsylvania, because war needs ships and iron; they went to the automobiles of Detroit and the load-carrying of Chicago; and they went to East St. Louis.

Now there came fear in the hearts of the Unwise Men. It was not that their wages were lowered,—they went even higher. They received, not simply a living wage, but a wage that paid for some of the decencies, and, in East St. Louis, many of the indecencies of life. What they feared was not deprivation of the things they were used to and the shadow of poverty, but rather the definite death of their rising dreams. But if fear was new-born in the hearts of the Unwise Men, the black man was born in a house of fear; to him poverty of the ugliest and straitest type was father, mother, and blood-brother. He was slipping stealthily northward to escape hunger and insult, the hand of oppression, and the shadow of death.

Here, then, in the wide valley which Father Marquette saw peaceful and golden, lazy with fruit and river, half-asleep beneath the nod of God,—here, then, was staged every element for human tragedy, every element of the modern economic paradox.

Ah! That hot, wide plain of East St. Louis is a gripping thing. The rivers are dirty with sweat and toil and lip, like lakes, along the low and burdened shores; flatboats ramble and thread among them, and above the steamers bridges swing on great arches of steel, striding with mighty grace from shore to shore. Everywhere are brick kennels,—tall, black and red chimneys, tongues of flame. The ground is littered with cars and iron, tracks and trucks, boxes and crates, metals and coal and rubber. Nature-defying cranes, grim elevators rise above pile on pile of black and grimy lumber. And ever below is the water,—wide and silent, gray-brown and yellow.

This is the stage for the tragedy: the armored might of the modern world urged by the bloody needs of the world wants, fevered today by a fabulous vision of gain and needing only hands, hands, hands! Fear of loss and greed of gain in the hearts of the giants; the clustered cunning of the modern workman, skilled as artificer and skilled in the rhythm of the habit of work, tasting the world's good and panting for more; fear of poverty and hate of "scabs" in the hearts of the workers; the dumb yearning in the hearts of the oppressed; the echo of laughter heard at the foot of the Pyramids; the faithful, plodding slouch of the laborers; fear of the Shadow of Death in the hearts of black men.

We ask, and perhaps there is no answer, how far may the captain of the world's industry do his deeds, despite the grinding tragedy of its doing? How far may men fight for the beginning of comfort, out beyond the horrid shadow of poverty, at the cost of starving other and what the world calls lesser men? How far may those who reach up out of the slime that fills the pits of the world's damned compel men with loaves to divide with men who starve?

The answers to these questions are hard, but yet one answer looms above all,—justice lies with the lowest; the plight of the lowest man,—the plight of the black man—deserves the first answer, and the plight of the giants of industry, the last.

Little cared East St. Louis for all this bandying of human problems, so long as its grocers and saloon-keepers flourished and its industries steamed and screamed and smoked and its bankers grew rich. Stupidity, license, and graft sat enthroned in the City Hall. The new black folk were exploited as cheerfully as white Polacks and Italians; the rent of shacks mounted merrily, the street car lines counted gleeful gains, and the crimes of white men and black men flourished in the dark. The high and skilled and smart climbed on the bent backs of the ignorant; harder the mass of laborers strove to unionize their fellows and to bargain with employers.

Nor were the new blacks fools. They had no love for nothings in labor; they had no wish to make their fellows' wage envelopes smaller, but they were determined to make their own larger. They, too, were willing to join in the new union movement. But the unions did not want them. Just as employers monopolized meat and steel, so they sought to monopolize labor and beat a giant's bargain. In the higher trades they succeeded. The best electrician in the city was refused admittance to the union and driven from the town because he was black. No black builder, printer, or machinist could join a union or work in East St. Louis, no matter what his skill or character. But out of the stink of the stockyards and the dust of the aluminum works and the sweat of the lumber yards the willing blacks could not be kept.

They were invited to join unions of the laborers here and they joined. White workers and black workers struck at the aluminum works in the fall and won higher wages and better hours; then again in the spring they struck to make bargaining compulsory for the employer, but this time they fronted new things. The conflagration of war had spread to America; government and court stepped in and ordered no hesitation, no strikes; the work must go on.

Deeper was the call for workers. Black men poured in and red anger flamed in the hearts of the white workers. The anger was against the wielders of the thunderbolts, but here it was impotent because employers stood with the hand of the government before their faces; it was against entrenched union labor, which had risen on the backs of the unskilled and unintelligent and on the backs of those whom for any reason of race or prejudice or chicane they could beat beyond the bars of competition; and finally the anger of the mass of white workers was turned toward these new black interlopers, who seemed to come to spoil their last dream of a great monopoly of common labor.

These angers flamed and the union leaders, fearing their fury and knowing their own guilt, not only in the larger and subtler matter of bidding their way to power across the weakness of their less fortunate fellows, but also conscious of their part in making East St. Louis a miserable town of liquor and lust, leaped quickly to ward the gathering thunder from their own heads. The thing they wanted was even at their hands: here were black men, guilty not only of bidding for jobs which white men could have held at war prices, even if they could not fill, but also guilty of being black! It was at this blackness that the unions pointed the accusing finger. It was here that they committed the unpardonable crime. It was here that they entered the Shadow of

Hell, where suddenly from a fight for wage and protection against industrial oppression East St. Louis became the center of the oldest and nastiest form of human oppression,—race hatred.

The whole situation lent itself to this terrible transformation. Everything in the history of the United States, from slavery to Sunday supplements, from disfranchisement to residence segregation, from "Jim-Crow" cars to a "Jim-Crow" army draft—all this history of discrimination and insult festered to make men think and willing to think that the venting of their unbridled anger against 12,000,000 humble, upstriving workers was a way of settling the industrial tangle of the ages. It was the logic of the broken plate, which, seared of old across its pattern, cracks never again, save along the old destruction.

So hell flamed in East St. Louis! The white men drove even black union men out of their unions and when the black men, beaten by night and assaulted, flew to arms and shot back at the marauders, five thousand rioters arose and surged like a crested stormwave, from noonday until midnight; they killed and beat and murdered; they dashed out the brains of children and stripped off the clothes of women; they drove victims into the flames and hanged the helpless to the lighting poles. Fathers were killed before the faces of mothers; children were burned; heads were cut off with axes; pregnant women crawled and spawned in dark, wet fields; thieves went through houses and firebrands followed; bodies were thrown from bridges; and rocks and bricks flew through the air.

The Negroes fought. They grappled with the mob like beasts at bay. They drove them back from the thickest cluster of their homes and piled the white dead on the street, but the cunning mob caught the black men between the factories and their homes, where they knew they were armed only with their dinner pails. Firemen, policemen, and militiamen stood with hanging hands or even joined eagerly with the mob.

It was the old world horror come to life again: all that Jews suffered in Spain and Poland; all that peasants suffered in France, and Indians in Calcutta; all that aroused human deviltry had accomplished in ages past they did in East St. Louis, while the rags of six thousand half-naked black men and women fluttered across the bridges of the calm Mississippi.

The white South laughed,—it was infinitely funny—the "niggers" who had gone North to escape slavery and lynching had met the fury of the mob which they had fled. Delegations rushed North from Mississippi and Texas, with suspicious timeliness and with great-hearted offers to take these workers back to a lesser hell. The man from Greensville, Mississippi, who wanted a thousand got six, because, after all, the end was not so simple.

No, the end was not simple. On the contrary, the problem raised by East St. Louis was curiously complex. The ordinary American, tired—of the persistence of "the Negro problem," sees only another anti-Negro mob and wonders, not when we shall settle this problem, but when we shall be well rid of it. The student of social things sees another mile-post in the triumphant march of union labor; he is sorry that blood and rapine should mark its march,— but, what will you? War is life!

Despite these smug reasonings the bare facts were these: East St. Louis, a great industrial center, lost 5,000 laborers,—good, honest, hard-working laborers. It was not the criminals, either black or white, who were driven from East St. Louis. They are still there. They will stay there. But half the honest black laborers were gone. The crippled

ranks of industrial organization in the mid-Mississippi
Valley cannot be recruited from Ellis Island, because in
Europe men are dead and maimed, and restoration, when
restoration comes, will raise a European demand for labor
such as this age has never seen. The vision of industrial
supremacy has come to the giants who lead American
industry and finance. But it can never be realized unless the
laborers are here to do the work,—the skilled laborers, the
common laborers, the willing laborers, the well-paid
laborers. The present forces, organized however cunningly,
are not large enough to do what America wants; but there
is another group of laborers, 12,000,000 strong, the natural
heirs, by every logic of justice, to the fruits of America's
industrial advance. They will be used simply because they
must be used,—but their using means East St. Louis!

Eastward from St. Louis lie great centers, like Chicago,
Indianapolis, Detroit, Cleveland, Pittsburg, Philadelphia,
and New York; in every one of these and in lesser centers
there is not only the industrial unrest of war and revolu-
tionized work, but there is the call for workers, the coming
of black folk, and the deliberate effort to divert the thoughts
of men, and particularly of workingmen, into channels of
race hatred against blacks. In every one of these centers
what happened in East St. Louis has been attempted, with
more or less success. Yet the American Negroes stand today
as the greatest strategic group in the world. Their services
are indispensable, their temper and character are fine, and
their souls have seen a vision more beautiful than any other
mass of workers. They may win back culture to the world
if their strength can be used with the forces of the world
that make for justice and not against the hidden hates that
fight for barbarism. For fight they must and fight they will!

Rising on wings we cross again the rivers of St. Louis,

winding and threading between the towers of industry that
threaten and drown the towers of God. Far, far beyond, we
sight the green of fields and hills; but ever below lies the
river, blue,—brownish-gray, touched with the hint of
hidden gold. Drifting through half-flooded lowlands, with
shanties and crops and stunted trees, past struggling corn and
straggling village, we rush toward the Battle of the Marne
and the West, from this dread Battle of the East. Westward,
dear God, the fire of Thy Mad World crimsons our Heaven.
Our answering Hell rolls eastward from St. Louis.

Here, in microcosm, is the sort of economic snarl that
arose continually for me and my pupils to solve. We could
bring to its unraveling little of the scholarly aloofness and
academic calm of most white universities. To us this thing
was Life and Hope and Death!

How should we think such a problem through, not
simply as Negroes, but as men and women of a new century, helping to build a new world? And first of all, here is
no simple question of race antagonism. There are no races,
in the sense of great, separate, pure breeds of men, differing
in attainment, development, and capacity. There are great
groups,—now with common history, now with common
interests, now with common ancestry; more and more
common experience and present interest drive back the
common blood and the world today consists, not of races,
but of the imperial commercial group of master capitalists,
international and predominantly white; the national middle
classes of the several nations, white, yellow, and brown, with
strong blood bonds, common languages, and common history; the international laboring class of all colors; the backward, oppressed groups of nature-folk, predominantly
yellow, brown, and black.

Two questions arise from the work and relations of

these groups: how to furnish goods and services for the
wants of men and how equitably and sufficiently to satisfy
these wants. There can be no doubt that we have passed in
our day from a world that could hardly satisfy the physical
wants of the mass of men, by the greatest effort, to a world
whose technique supplies enough for all, if all can claim
their right. Our great ethical question today is, therefore,
how may we justly distribute the world's goods to satisfy the
necessary wants of the mass of men.

What hinders the answer to this question? Dislikes, jealousies, hatreds,—undoubtedly like the race hatred in East
St. Louis; the jealousy of English and German; the dislike of
the Jew and the Gentile. But these are, after all, surface dis-
turbances, sprung from ancient habit more than from present reason. They persist and are encouraged because of
deeper, mightier currents. If the white workingmen of East
St. Louis felt sure that Negro workers would not and could
not take the bread and cake from their mouths, their race
hatred would never have been translated into murder. If the
black workingmen of the South could earn a decent living
under decent circumstances at home, they would not be
compelled to underbid their white fellows.

Thus the shadow of hunger, in a world which never
needs to be hungry, drives us to war and murder and hate.
But why does hunger shadow so vast a mass of men? Manifestly because in the great organizing of men for work a
few of the participants come out with more wealth than
they can possibly use, while a vast number emerge with less
than can decently support life. In earlier economic stages we
defended this as the reward of Thrift and Sacrifice, and as
the punishment of Ignorance and Crime. To this the answer
is sharp: Sacrifice calls for no such reward and Ignorance
deserves no such punishment. The chief meaning of our

present thinking is that the disproportion between wealth and poverty today cannot be adequately accounted for by the thrift and ignorance of the rich and the poor.

Yesterday we righted one great mistake when we realized that the ownership of the laborer did not tend to increase production. The world at large had learned this long since, but black slavery arose again in America as an inexplicable anachronism, a wilful crime. The freeing of the black slaves freed America. Today we are challenging another ownership,—the ownership of materials which go to make the goods we need. Private ownership of land, tools, and raw materials may at one stage of economic development be a method of stimulating production and one which does not greatly interfere with equitable distribution. When, however, the intricacy and length of technical production increased, the ownership of these things becomes a monopoly, which easily makes the rich richer and the poor poorer. Today, therefore, we are challenging this ownership; we are demanding general consent as to what materials shall be privately owned and as to how materials shall be used. We are rapidly approaching the day when we shall repudiate all private property in raw materials and tools and demand that distribution hinge, not on the power of those who monopolize the materials, but on the needs of the mass of men.

Can we do this and still make sufficient goods, justly gauge the needs of men, and rightly decide who are to be considered "men"? How do we arrange to accomplish these things today? Somebody decides whose wants should be satisfied. Somebody organizes industry so as to satisfy these wants. What is to hinder the same ability and foresight from being used in the future as in the past? The amount and kind of human ability necessary need not be decreased,—it may even be vastly increased, with proper encouragement and rewards. Are we today evoking the necessary ability? On the contrary, it is not the Inventor, the Manager, and the Thinker who today are reaping the great rewards of industry, but rather the Gambler and the Highwayman. Rightly-organized industry might easily save the Gambler's Profit and the Monopolist's Interest and by paying a more discriminating reward in wealth and honor bring to the service of the state more ability and sacrifice than we can today command. If we do away with interest and profit, consider the savings that could be made; but above all, think how great the revolution would be when we ask the mysterious Somebody to decide in the light of public opinion whose wants should be satisfied. This is the great and real revolution that is coming in future industry.

But this is not the end of the revolution nor indeed, perhaps, its real beginning. What we must decide sometime is who are to be considered "men." Today, at the beginning of this industrial change, we are admitting that economic classes must give way. The laborers' hire must increase, the employers' profit must be curbed. But how far shall this change go? Must it apply to all human beings and to all work throughout the world?

Certainly not. We seek to apply it slowly and with some reluctance to white men and more slowly and with greater reserve to white women, but black folk and brown and for the most part yellow folk we have widely determined shall not be among those whose needs must justly be heard and whose wants must be ministered to in the great organization of world industry.

In the teaching of my classes I was not willing to stop with showing that this was unfair,—indeed I did not have to do this. They knew through bitter experience its rank injustice, because they were black. What I had to show was that no real reorganization of industry could be permanently made with the majority of mankind left out. These disinherited darker peoples must either share in the future industrial democracy or overturn the world.

Of course, the foundation of such a system must be a high, ethical ideal. We must really envisage the wants of humanity. We must want the wants of all men. We must get rid of the fascination for exclusiveness. Here, in a world full of folk, men are lonely. The rich are lonely. We are all frantic for fellow-souls, yet we shut souls out and bar the ways and bolster up the fiction of the Elect and the Superior when the great mass of men is capable of producing larger and larger numbers for every human height of attainment. To be sure, there are differences between men and groups and there will ever be, but they will be differences of beauty and genius and of interest and not necessarily of ugliness, imbecility, and hatred.

The meaning of America is the beginning of the discovery of the Crowd. The crowd is not so well-trained as a Versailles garden party of Louis XIV, but it is far better trained than the Sans-culottes and it has infinite possibilities. What a world this will be when human possibilities are freed, when we discover each other, when the stranger is no longer the potential criminal and the certain inferior!

What hinders our approach to the ideals outlined above? Our profit from degradation, our colonial exploitation, our American attitude toward the Negro. Think again of East St. Louis! Think back of that to slavery and Reconstruction! Do we want the wants of American Negroes satisfied? Most certainly not, and that negative is the greatest hindrance today to the reorganization of work and redistribution of wealth, not only in America, but in the world.

All humanity must share in the future industrial democracy of the world. For this it must be trained in intelligence and in appreciation of the good and the beautiful. Present Big Business,—that Science of Human Wants—must be perfected by eliminating the price paid for waste, which is Interest, and for Chance, which is Profit, and making all income a personal wage for service rendered by the recipient; by recognizing no possible human service as great enough to enable a person to designate another as an idler or as a worker at work which he cannot do. Above all, industry must minister to the wants of the many and not to the few, and the Negro, the Indian, the Mongolian, and the South Sea Islander must be among the many as well as Germans, Frenchmen, and Englishmen.

In this coming socialization of industry we must guard against that same tyranny of the majority that has marked democracy in the making of laws. There must, for instance, persist in this future economics a certain minimum of machine-like work and prompt obedience and submission. This necessity is a simple corollary from the hard facts of the physical world. It must be accepted with the comforting thought that its routine need not demand twelve hours a day or even eight. With Work for All and All at Work probably from three to six hours would suffice, and leave abundant time for leisure, exercise, study, and avocations.

But what shall we say of work where spiritual values and social distinctions enter? Who shall be Artists and who shall be Servants in the world to come? Or shall we all be artists and all serve?

The Second Coming

Three bishops sat in San Francisco, New Orleans, and New York, peering gloomily into three flickering fires, which cast and recast shuddering shadows on book-lined walls. Three letters lay in their laps, which said:

"And thou, Valdosta, in the land of Georgia, art not least among the princes of America, for out of thee shall come a governor who shall rule my people."

The white bishop of New York scowled and impatiently threw the letter into the fire. "Valdosta?" he thought, —"That's where I go to the governor's wedding of little Marguerite, my white flower,—" Then he forgot the writing in his musing, but the paper flared red in the fireplace.

"Valdosta?" said the black bishop of New Orleans, turning uneasily in his chair. "I must go down there. Those colored folk are acting strangely. I don't know where all this unrest and moving will lead to. Then, there's poor Lucy—" And he threw the letter into the fire, but eyed it suspiciously as it flamed green. "Stranger things than that have happened," he said slowly, " 'and ye shall hear of wars and rumors of wars . . . for nation shall rise against nation and kingdom against kingdom.' "

In San Francisco the priest of Japan, abroad to study strange lands, sat in his lacquer chair, with face like soft-yellow and wrinkled parchment. Slowly he wrote in a great and golden book: "I have been strangely bidden to the Val d' Osta, where one of those religious cults that swarm here will welcome a prophet. I shall go and report to Kioto."

So in the dim waning of the day before Christmas three bishops met in Valdosta and saw its mills and storehouses, its wide-throated and sandy streets, in the mellow glow of a crimson sun. The governor glared anxiously up the street as he helped the bishop of New York into his car and welcomed him graciously.

"I am troubled," said the governor, "about the niggers. They are acting queerly. I'm not certain but Fleming is back of it."

"Fleming?"

"Yes! He's running against me next term for governor; he's a fire-brand; wants niggers to vote and all that—pardon me a moment, there's a darky I know—" and he hurried to the black bishop, who had just descended from the "Jim-Crow" car, and clasped his hand cordially. They talked in whispers. "Search diligently," said the governor in parting, "and bring me word again." Then returning to his guest, "You will excuse me, won't you?" he asked, "but I am sorely troubled! I never saw niggers act so. They're leaving by the hundreds and those who stay are getting impudent! They seem to be expecting something. What's the crowd, Jim?"

The chauffeur said that there was some sort of Chinese official in town and everybody wanted to glimpse him. He drove around another way.

It all happened very suddenly. The bishop of New York, in full canonicals for the early wedding, stepped out on the rear balcony of his mansion, just as the dying sun lit crimson clouds of glory in the East and burned the West.

"Fire!" yelled a wag in the surging crowd that was gathering to celebrate a southern Christmas-eve; all laughed and ran.

The bishop of New York did not understand. He peered around. Was it that dark, little house in the far backyard that flamed? Forgetful of his robes, he hurried down,—a brave, white figure in the sunset. He found himself before an old, black, rickety stable. He could hear the mules stamping within.

No. It was not fire. It was the sunset glowing through the cracks. Behind the hut its glory rose toward God like flaming wings of cherubim. He paused until he heard the faint wail of a child. Hastily he entered. A white girl crouched before him, down by the very mules' feet, with a baby in her arms,—a little mite of a baby that wailed weakly. Behind mother and child stood a shadow. The bishop of New York turned to the right, inquiringly, and saw a black man in bishop's robes that faintly re-echoed his own. He turned away to the left and saw a golden Japanese in golden garb. Then he heard the black man mutter behind him: "But He was to come the second time in clouds of glory, with the nations gathered around Him and angels—" at the word a shaft of glorious light fell full upon the child, while without came the tramping of unnumbered feet and the whirring of wings.

The bishop of New York bent quickly over the baby. *It was black!* He stepped back with a gesture of disgust, hardly listening to and yet hearing the black bishop, who spoke almost as if in apology:

"She's not really white; I know Lucy—you see, her mother worked for the governor—" The white bishop turned on his heel and nearly trod on the yellow priest, who knelt with bowed head before the pale mother and offered incense and a gift of gold.

Out into the night rushed the bishop of New York. The wings of the cherubim were folded black against the stars. As he hastened down the front staircase the governor came rushing up the street steps.

"We are late!" he cried nervously. "The bride awaits!" He hurried the bishop to the waiting limousine, asking him anxiously: "Did you hear anything? Do you hear that noise? The crowd is growing strangely on the streets and there seems to be a fire over toward the East. I never saw so many people here—I fear violence—a mob—a lynching—I fear—hark!"

What was that which he, too, heard beneath the rhythm of unnumbered feet? Deep in his heart a wonder grew. What was it? Ah, he knew! It was music,—some strong and mighty chord. It rose higher as the brilliantly-lighted church split the night, and swept radiantly toward them. So high and clear that music flew, it seemed above, around, behind them. The governor, ashen-faced, crouched in the car; but the bishop said softly as the ecstasy pulsed in his heart:

"Such music, such wedding music! What choir is it?"

V | "THE SERVANT IN THE HOUSE"

The lady looked at me severely; I glanced away. I had addressed the little audience at some length on the disfranchisement of my people in society, politics, and industry and had studiously avoided the while her cold, green eye. I finished and shook weary hands, while she lay in wait. I knew what was coming and braced my soul.

"Do you know where I can get a good colored cook?" she asked.

I disclaimed all guilty concupiscence. She came nearer and spitefully shook a finger in my face.

"Why—won't—Negroes—work!" she panted. "I have given money for years to Hampton and Tuskegee and yet I can't get decent servants. They won't try. They're lazy! They're unreliable! They're impudent and they leave without notice. They all want to be lawyers and doctors and" (she spat the word in venom) "ladies!"

"God forbid!" I answered solemnly, and then being of gentle birth and unminded to strike a defenseless female of uncertain years, I ran; I ran home and wrote a chapter in my book and this is it.

I speak and speak bitterly as a servant and a servant's son, for my mother spent five or more years of her life as a menial; my father's family escaped, although grandfather as a boat steward had to fight hard to be a man and not a lackey. He fought and won. My mother's folk, however, during my childhood, sat poised on that thin edge between the farmer and the menial. The surrounding Irish had two chances, the factory and the kitchen, and most of them took the factory, with all its dirt and noise and low wage. The factory was closed to us. Our little lands were too small to feed most of us. A few clung almost sullenly to the old homes, low and red things crouching on a wide level; but the children stirred restlessly and walked often to town and saw its wonders. Slowly they dribbled off,—a waiter here, a cook there, help for a few weeks in Mrs. Blank's kitchen when she had summer boarders.

Instinctively I hated such work from my birth. I loathed it and shrank from it. Why? I could not have said. Had I been born in Carolina instead of Massachusetts I should hardly have escaped the taint of "service." Its temptations in wage and comfort would soon have answered my scruples; and yet I am sure I would have fought long even in Carolina, for I knew in my heart that thither lay Hell.

I mowed lawns on contract, did "chores" that left me my own man, sold papers, and peddled tea—anything to escape the shadow of the awful thing that lurked to grip my soul. Once, and once only, I felt the sting of its talons. I was twenty and had graduated from Fisk with a scholarship for Harvard; I needed, however, travel money and clothes and a bit to live on until the scholarship was due. Fortson was a fellow-student in winter and a waiter in summer. He proposed that the Glee Club Quartet of Fisk spend the summer at the hotel in Minnesota where he worked and that I go along as "Business Manager" to arrange for engagements on the journey back. We were all eager, but we knew nothing of table-waiting. "Never mind," said Fortson, "you can stand around the dining-room during meals and carry out the big wooden trays of dirty dishes. Thus you can pick up knowledge of waiting and earn good tips and get free board." I listened askance, but I went.

I entered that broad and blatant hotel at Lake Minnetonka with distinct forebodings. The flamboyant architecture, the great verandas, rich furniture, and richer dresses awed us mightily. The long loft reserved for us, with its clean little cots, was reassuring; the work was not difficult,—but the meals! There were no meals. At first, before the guests ate, a dirty table in the kitchen was hastily strewn with uneatable scraps. We novices were the only ones who came to eat, while the guests' dining-room, with its savors and sights, set our appetites on edge! After a while even the pretense of meals for us was dropped. We were sure we were going to starve when Dug, one of us, made a startling discovery: the waiters stole their food and they stole the best. We gulped and hesitated. Then we stole, too, (or, at least, they stole and I shared) and we all fattened, for the dainties were marvelous. You slipped a bit here and hid it there; you cut off extra portions and gave false orders; you dashed off into darkness and hid in corners and ate and ate! It was nasty business. I hated it. I was too cowardly to steal much myself, and not coward enough to refuse what others stole.

Our work was easy, but insipid. We stood about and watched overdressed people gorge. For the most part we were treated like furniture and were supposed to act the wooden part. I watched the waiters even more than the guests. I saw that it paid to amuse and to cringe. One particular black man set me crazy. He was intelligent and deft, but one day I caught sight of his face as he served a crowd of men; he was playing the clown,—crouching, grinning, assuming a broad dialect when he usually spoke good English—ah! it was a heartbreaking sight, and he made more money than any waiter in the dining-room.

I did not mind the actual work or the kind of work, but it was the dishonesty and deception, the flattery and cajolery, the unnatural assumption that worker and diner had no common humanity. It was uncanny. It was inherently and fundamentally wrong. I stood staring and thinking, while the other boys hustled about. Then I noticed one fat hog, feeding at a heavily gilded trough, who could not find his waiter. He beckoned me. It was not his voice, for his mouth was too full. It was his way, his air, his assumption. Thus Caesar ordered his legionaries or Cleopatra her slaves. Dogs recognized the gesture. I did not. He may be beckoning yet for all I know, for something froze within me. I did not look his way again. Then and there I disowned menial service for me and my people.

I would work my hands off for an honest wage, but for "tips" and "hand-me-outs," never! Fortson was a pious, honest fellow, who regarded "tips" as in the nature of things, being to the manner born; but the hotel that summer in other respects rather astonished even him. He came to us much flurried one night and got us to help him with a memorial to the absentee proprietor, telling of the wild and gay doings of midnights in the rooms and corridors among "tired" business men and their prostitutes. We listened wide-eyed and eager and wrote the filth out manfully. The proprietor did not thank Fortson. He did not even answer the letter.

When I finally walked out of that hotel and out of menial service forever, I felt as though, in a field of flowers, my nose had been held unpleasantly long to the worms and manure at their roots.

"Cursed be Canaan!" cried the Hebrew priests. "A servant of servants shall he be unto his brethren." With what characteristic complacency did the slaveholders assume that Canaanites were Negroes and their "brethren" white? Are not Negroes servants? *Ergo!* Upon such spiritual myths was the anachronism of American slavery built, and this was the degradation that once made menial servants the aristocrats among colored folk. House servants secured some decencies of food and clothing and shelter; they could more easily reach their master's ear; their personal abilities of character became known and bonds grew between slave and master which strengthened from friendship to love, from mutual service to mutual blood.

Naturally out of this the West Indian servant climbed out of slavery into citizenship, for few West Indian masters—fewer Spanish or Dutch—were callous enough to sell their own children into slavery. Not so with English and Americans. With a harshness and indecency seldom paralleled in the civilized world white masters on the mainland sold their mulatto children, half-brothers and half-sisters, and their own wives in all but name, into life-slavery by the hundreds and thousands. They originated a special branch of slave-trading for this trade and the white aristocrats of Virginia and the Carolinas made more money by this business during the eighteenth and nineteenth centuries than in any other way.

The clang of the door of opportunity thus knelled in the ears of the colored house servant whirled the whole face of Negro advancement as on some great pivot. The movement was slow, but vast. When emancipation came, before and after 1863, the house servant still held advantages. He had whatever education the race possessed and his white father, no longer able to sell him, often helped him with land and protection. Notwithstanding this the lure of house service for the Negro was gone. The path of salvation for the emancipated host of black folk lay no longer through the kitchen door, with its wide hall and pillared veranda and flowered yard beyond. It lay, as every Negro soon knew and knows, in escape from menial serfdom.

In 1860, 98 percent of the Negroes were servants and serfs. In 1880, 30 percent were servants and 65 percent were serfs. The percentage of servants then rose slightly and fell again until 21 percent were in service in 1910 and, doubtless, much less than 20 percent today. This is the measure of our rise, but the Negro will not approach freedom until this hateful badge of slavery and mediaevalism has been reduced to less than 10 percent.

Not only are less than a fifth of our workers servants today, but the character of their service has been changed. The million menial workers among us include 300,000 upper servants,—skilled men and women of character, like hotel waiters, Pullman porters, janitors, and cooks, who, had they been white, could have called on the great labor movement to lift their work out of slavery, to standardize their hours, to define their duties, and to substitute a living, regular wage for personal largess in the shape of tips, old clothes, and cold leavings of food. But the labor movement turned their backs on those black men when the white world dinned in their ears. *Negroes are servants; servants are Negroes.* They shut the door of escape to factory and trade in their fellows' faces and battened down the hatches, lest the 300,000 should be workers equal in pay and consideration with white men.

But, if the upper servants could not escape to modern,

industrial conditions, how much the more did they press down on the bodies and souls of 700,000 washerwomen and household drudges,—ignorant, unskilled offal of a millionaire industrial system. Their pay was the lowest and their hours the longest of all workers. The personal degradation of their work is so great that any white man of decency would rather cut his daughter's throat than let her grow up to such a destiny. There is throughout the world and in all races no greater source of prostitution than this grade of menial service, and the Negro race in America has largely escaped this destiny simply because its innate decency leads black women to choose irregular and temporary sexual relations with men they like rather than to sell themselves to strangers. To such sexual morals is added (in the nature of self-defense) that revolt against unjust labor conditions which expresses itself in "soldiering," sullenness, petty pilfering, unreliability, and fast and fruitless changes of masters.

Indeed, here among American Negroes we have exemplified the last and worst refuge of industrial caste. Menial service is an anachronism,—the refuse of mediaeval barbarism. Why, then, does it linger? Why are we silent about it? Why in the minds of so many decent and up-seeing folks does the whole Negro problem resolve itself into the matter of their getting a cook or a maid?

No one knows better than I the capabilities of a system of domestic service at its best. I have seen children who were spiritual sons and daughters of their masters, girls who were friends of their mistresses, and old servants honored and revered. But in every such case the Servant had transcended the Menial, the Service had been exalted above the Wage. Now to accomplish this permanently and universally, calls for the same revolution in household help as in factory help and public service. While organized industry has been slowly making its help into self-respecting, well-paid men, and while public service is beginning to call for the highest types of educated and efficient thinkers, domestic service lags behind and insists upon seeking to evolve the best types of men from the worst conditions.

The cause of this perversity, to my mind, is twofold. First, the ancient high estate of Service, now pitifully fallen, yet gasping for breath; secondly, the present low estate of the outcasts of the world, peering with blood-shot eyes at the gates of the industrial heaven.

The Master spoke no greater word than that which said: "Whosoever will be great among you, let him be your servant!" What is greater than Personal Service! Surely no social service, no wholesale helping of masses of men can exist which does not find its effectiveness and beauty in the personal aid of man to man. It is the purest and holiest of duties. Some mighty glimmer of this truth survived in those who made the First Gentlemen of the Bedchamber, the Keepers of the Robes, and the Knights of the Bath, the highest nobility that hedged an anointed king. Nor does it differ today in what the mother does for the child or the daughter for the mother, in all the personal attentions in the old-fashioned home; this is Service! Think of what Friend has meant, not simply in spiritual sympathies, but in physical helpfulness. In the world today what calls for more of love, sympathy, learning, sacrifice, and long-suffering than the care of children, the preparation of food, the cleansing and ordering of the home, personal attendance and companionship, the care of bodies and their raiment—what greater, more intimate, more holy Services are there than these?

And yet we are degrading these services and loathing them and scoffing at them and spitting upon them, first, by turning them over to the lowest and least competent and worst trained classes in the world, and then by yelling like spoiled children if our babies are neglected, our biscuits sodden, our homes dirty, and our baths unpoured. Let one suggest that the only cure for such deeds is in the uplift of the doer and our rage is even worse and less explicable. We will call them by their first names, thus blaspheming a holy intimacy; we will confine them to back doors; we will insist that their meals be no gracious ceremony nor even a restful sprawl, but usually a hasty, heckled gulp amid garbage; we exact, not a natural, but a purchased deference, and we leave them naked to insult by our children and by our husbands.

I remember a girl,—how pretty she was, with the crimson flooding the old ivory of her cheeks and her gracious plumpness! She had come to the valley during the summer to "do housework." I met and walked home with her, in the thrilling shadows, to an old village home I knew well; then as I turned to leave I learned that she was there alone in that house for a week-end with only one young white man to represent the family. Oh, he was doubtless a "gentleman" and all that, but for the first time in my life I saw what a snare the fowler was spreading at the feet of the daughters of my people, baited by church and state.

Not alone is the hurt thus offered to the lowly,— Society and Science suffer. The unit which we seek to make the center of society,—the Home—is deprived of the help of scientific invention and suggestion. It is only slowly and by the utmost effort that some small foothold has been gained for the vacuum cleaner, the washing-machine, the power tool, and the chemical reagent. In our frantic effort to preserve the last vestiges of slavery and mediaevalism we not only set our faces against such improvements, but we seek to use education and the power of the state to train the servants who do not naturally appear.

Meantime the wild rush from house service, on the part of all who can scramble or run, continues. The rules of the labor union are designed, not simply to raise wages, but to guard against any likeness between artisan and servant. There is no essential difference in ability and training between a subway guard and a Pullman porter, but between their union cards lies a whole world.

Yet we are silent. Menial service is not a "social problem." It is not really discussed. There is no scientific program for its "reform." There is but one panacea: Escape! Get yourselves and your sons and daughters out of the shadow of this awful thing! Hire servants, but never be one. Indeed, subtly but surely the ability to hire at least "a maid" is still civilization's patent to respectability, while "a man" is the first word of aristocracy.

All this is because we still consciously and unconsciously hold to the "manure" theory of social organization. We believe that at the bottom of organized human life there are necessary duties and services which no real human being ought to be compelled to do. We push below this mudsill the derelicts and half-men, whom we hate and despise, and seek to build above it—Democracy! On such foundations is reared a Theory of Exclusiveness, a feeling that the world progresses by a process of excluding from the benefits of culture the majority of men, so that a gifted minority may blossom. Through this door the modern democrat arrives to the place where he is willing to allot two able-bodied men and two fine horses to the task of helping one wizened beldam to take the morning air.

Here the absurdity ends. Here all honest minds turn back and ask: Is menial service permanent or necessary? Can we not transfer cooking from the home to the scientific laboratory, along with the laundry? Cannot machinery, in the hands of self-respecting and well-paid artisans, do our cleaning, sewing, moving, and decorating? Cannot the training of children become an even greater profession than the attending of the sick? And cannot personal service and companionship be coupled with friendship and love where it belongs and whence it can never be divorced without degradation and pain?

In fine, can we not, black and white, rich and poor, look forward to a world of Service without Servants?

A miracle! you say? True. And only to be performed by the Immortal Child.

Jesus Christ in Texas

It was in Waco, Texas.

The convict guard laughed. "I don't know," he said, "I hadn't thought of that." He hesitated and looked at the stranger curiously. In the solemn twilight he got an impression of unusual height and soft, dark eyes. "Curious sort of acquaintance for the colonel," he thought; then he continued aloud: "But that nigger there is bad, a born thief, and ought to be sent up for life; got ten years last time—"

Here the voice of the promoter, talking within, broke in; he was bending over his figures, sitting by the colonel. He was slight, with a sharp nose.

"The convicts," he said, "would cost us $96 a year and board. Well, we can squeeze this so that it won't be over $125 apiece. Now if these fellows are driven, they can build this line within twelve months. It will be running by next April. Freights will fall fifty percent. Why, man, you'll be a millionaire in less than ten years."

The colonel started. He was a thick, short man, with a clean-shaven face and a certain air of breeding about the lines of his countenance; the word millionaire sounded well to his ears. He thought—he thought a great deal; he almost heard the puff of the fearfully costly automobile that was coming up the road, and he said:

"I suppose we might as well hire them."

"Of course," answered the promoter.

The voice of the tall stranger in the corner broke in here:

"It will be a good thing for them?" he said, half in question.

The colonel moved. "The guard makes strange friends," he thought to himself. "What's this man doing here, anyway?" He looked at him, or rather looked at his eyes, and then somehow he felt a warming toward him. He said:

"Well, at least, it can't harm them; they're beyond that."

"It will do them good, then," said the stranger again.

The promoter shrugged his shoulders. "It will do us good," he said.

But the colonel shook his head impatiently. He felt a desire to justify himself before those eyes, and he answered: "Yes, it will do them good; or at any rate it won't make them any worse than they are." Then he started to say something else, but here sure enough the sound of the automobile breathing at the gate stopped him and they all arose.

"It is settled, then," said the promoter.

"Yes," said the colonel, turning toward the stranger again. "Are you going into town?" he asked with the Southern courtesy of white men to white men in a country town. The stranger said he was. "Then come along in my machine. I want to talk with you about this."

They went out to the car. The stranger as he went turned again to look back at the convict. He was a tall, powerfully built black fellow. His face was sullen, with a low forehead, thick, hanging lips, and bitter eyes. There was revolt written about his mouth despite the hangdog expression. He stood bending over his pile of stones, pounding listlessly. Beside him stood a boy of twelve,—yellow, with a hunted, crafty look. The convict raised his eyes and they met the eyes of the stranger. The hammer fell from his hands.

The stranger turned slowly toward the automobile and the colonel introduced him. He had not exactly caught his name, but he mumbled something as he presented him to his wife and little girl, who were waiting.

As they whirled away the colonel started to talk, but the stranger had taken the little girl into his lap and together they conversed in low tones all the way home.

In some way, they did not exactly know how, they got the impression that the man was a teacher and, of course, he must be a foreigner. The long, cloak-like coat told this. They rode in the twilight through the lighted town and at last drew up before the colonel's mansion, with its ghost-like pillars.

The lady in the back seat was thinking of the guests she had invited to dinner and was wondering if she ought not to ask this man to stay. He seemed cultured and she supposed he was some acquaintance of the colonel's. It would be rather interesting to have him there, with the judge's wife and daughter and the rector. She spoke almost before she thought:

"You will enter and rest awhile?"

The colonel and the little girl insisted. For a moment the stranger seemed about to refuse. He said he had some business for his father, about town. Then for the child's sake he consented.

Up the steps they went and into the dark parlor where they sat and talked a long time. It was a curious conversation. Afterwards they did not remember exactly what was said and yet they all remembered a certain strange satisfaction in that long, low talk.

Finally the nurse came for the reluctant child and the hostess bethought herself:

"We will have a cup of tea; you will be dry and tired."

She rang and switched on a blaze of light. With one accord they all looked at the stranger, for they had hardly seen him well in the glooming twilight. The woman started in amazement and the colonel half rose in anger. Why, the man was a mulatto, surely; even if he did not own the Negro blood, their practised eyes knew it. He was tall and straight and the coat looked like a Jewish gabardine. His hair hung in close curls far down the sides of his face and his face was olive, even yellow.

A peremptory order rose to the colonel's lips and froze there as he caught the stranger's eyes. Those eyes,—where had he seen those eyes before? He remembered them long years ago. The soft, tear-filled eyes of a brown girl. He remembered many things, and his face grew drawn and white. Those eyes kept burning into him, even when they were turned half away toward the staircase, where the white figure of the child hovered with her nurse and waved goodnight. The lady sank into her chair and thought: "What will the judge's wife say? How did the colonel come to invite this man here? How shall we be rid of him?" She looked at the colonel in reproachful consternation.

Just then the door opened and the old butler came in. He was an ancient black man, with tufted white hair, and he held before him a large, silver tray filled with a china tea service. The stranger rose slowly and stretched forth his hands as if to bless the viands. The old man paused in bewilderment, tottered, and then with sudden gladness in his eyes dropped to his knees, and the tray crashed to the floor.

"My Lord and my God!" he whispered; but the woman screamed: "Mother's china!"

The doorbell rang.

"Heavens! here is the dinner party!" exclaimed the lady. She turned toward the door, but there in the hail, clad in her night clothes, was the little girl. She had stolen down the stairs to see the stranger again, and the nurse above was calling in vain. The woman felt hysterical and scolded at the nurse, but the stranger had stretched out his arms and with a glad cry the child nestled in them. They caught some words about the "Kingdom of Heaven" as he slowly mounted the stairs with his little, white burden.

The mother was glad of anything to get rid of the interloper, even for a moment. The bell rang again and she hastened toward the door, which the loitering black maid was just opening. She did not notice the shadow of the stranger as he came slowly down the stairs and paused by the newel post, dark and silent.

The judge's wife came in. She was an old woman, frilled and powdered into a semblance of youth, and gorgeously gowned. She came forward, smiling with extended hands, but when she was opposite the stranger, somewhere a chill seemed to strike her and she shuddered and cried:

"What a draft!" as she drew a silken shawl about her and shook hands cordially; she forgot to ask who the stranger was. The judge strode in unseeing, thinking of a puzzling case of theft.

"Eh? What? Oh—er—yes,—good evening," he said, "good evening." Behind them came a young woman in the glory of youth, and daintily silked, beautiful in face and form, with diamonds around her fair neck. She came in lightly, but stopped with a little gasp; then she laughed gaily and said:

"Why, I beg your pardon. Was it not curious? I thought I saw there behind your man"—she hesitated, but he must be a servant, she argued—"the shadow of great, white wings. It was but the light on the drapery. What a turn it gave me." And she smiled again. With her came a tall, handsome, young naval officer. Hearing his lady refer to the servant, he hardly looked at him, but held his gilded cap carelessly toward him, and the stranger placed it carefully on the rack.

Last came the rector, a man of forty, and well-clothed. He started to pass the stranger, stopped, and looked at him inquiringly.

"I beg your pardon," he said. "I beg your pardon,—I think I have met you?"

The stranger made no answer, and the hostess nervously hurried the guests on. But the rector lingered and looked perplexed.

"Surely, I know you. I have met you somewhere," he said, putting his hand vaguely to his head. "You—you remember me, do you not?"

The stranger quietly swept his cloak aside, and to the hostess' unspeakable relief passed out of the door.

"I never knew you," he said in low tones as he went.

The lady murmured some vain excuse about intruders, but the rector stood with annoyance written on his face.

"I beg a thousand pardons," he said to the hostess absently. "It is a great pleasure to be here,—somehow I thought I knew that man. I am sure I knew him once."

The stranger had passed down the steps, and as he passed, the nurse, lingering at the top of the staircase, flew down after him, caught his cloak, trembled, hesitated, and then kneeled in the dust.

He touched her lightly with his hand and said: "Go, and sin no more!"

With a glad cry the maid left the house, with its open door, and turned north, running. The stranger turned eastward into the night. As they parted a long, low howl rose tremulously and reverberated through the night. The colonel's wife within shuddered.

"The bloodhounds!" she said.

The rector answered carelessly:

"Another one of those convicts escaped, I suppose.

Really, they need severer measures." Then he stopped. He was trying to remember that stranger's name.

The judge's wife looked about for the draft and arranged her shawl. The girl glanced at the white drapery in the hall, but the young officer was bending over her and the fires of life burned in her veins.

Howl after howl rose in the night, swelled, and died away. The stranger strode rapidly along the highway and out into the deep forest. There he paused and stood waiting, tall and still.

A mile up the road behind a man was running, tall and powerful and black, with crime-stained face and convicts' stripes upon him, and shackles on his legs. He ran and jumped, in little, short steps, and his chains rang. He fell and rose again, while the howl of the hounds rang louder behind him.

Into the forest he leapt and crept and jumped and ran, streaming with sweat; seeing the tall form rise before him, he stopped suddenly, dropped his hands in sullen impotence, and sank panting to the earth. A greyhound shot out of the woods behind him, howled, whined, and fawned before the stranger's feet. Hound after hound bayed, leapt, and lay there; then silently, one by one, and with bowed heads, they crept backward toward the town.

The stranger made a cup of his hands and gave the man water to drink, bathed his hot head, and gently took the chains and irons from his feet. By and by the convict stood up. Day was dawning above the treetops. He looked into the stranger's face, and for a moment a gladness swept over the stains of his face.

"Why, you are a nigger, too," he said.

Then the convict seemed anxious to justify himself.

"I never had no chance," he said furtively.

"Thou shalt not steal," said the stranger.

The man bridled.

"But how about them? Can they steal? Didn't they steal a whole year's work, and then when I stole to keep from starving————" He glanced at the stranger.

"No, I didn't steal just to keep from starving. I stole to be stealing. I can't seem to keep from stealing. Seems like when I see things, I just must—but, yes, I'll try!"

The convict looked down at his striped clothes, but the stranger had taken off his long coat; he had put it around him and the stripes disappeared.

In the opening morning the black man started toward the low, log farmhouse in the distance, while the stranger stood watching him. There was a new glory in the day. The black man's face cleared up, and the farmer was glad to get him. All day the black man worked as he had never worked before. The farmer gave him some cold food.

"You can sleep in the barn," he said, and turned away.

"How much do I git a day?" asked the black man.

The farmer scowled.

"Now see here," said he. "If you'll sign a contract for the season, I'll give you ten dollars a month."

"I won't sign no contract," said the black man doggedly.

"Yes, you will," said the farmer, threateningly, "or I'll call the convict guard." And he grinned.

The convict shrank and slouched to the barn. As night fell he looked out and saw the farmer leave the place. Slowly he crept out and sneaked toward the house. He looked through the kitchen door. No one was there, but the supper was spread as if the mistress had laid it and gone out. He ate ravenously. Then he looked into the front room and listened. He could hear low voices on the porch. On the table lay a gold watch. He gazed at it, and in a moment he was beside it,—his hands were on it! Quickly he slipped out of

the house and slouched toward the field. He saw his
employer coming along the highway. He fled back in terror
and around to the front of the house, when suddenly he
stopped. He felt the great, dark eyes of the stranger and saw
the same dark, cloak-like coat where the stranger sat on the
doorstep talking with the mistress of the house. Slowly,
guiltily, he turned back, entered the kitchen, and laid the
watch stealthily where he had found it; then he rushed
wildly back toward the stranger, with arms outstretched.

The woman had laid supper for her husband, and going
down from the house had walked out toward a neighbor's. She
was gone but a little while, and when she came back started
to see a dark figure on the doorsteps under the tall, red oak.
She thought it was the new Negro until he said in a soft voice:

"Will you give me bread?"

Reassured at the voice of a white man, she answered
quickly in her soft, Southern tones:

"Why, certainly."

She was a little woman, and once had been pretty; but
now her face was drawn with work and care. She was nervous and always thinking, wishing, wanting for something.
She went in and got him some cornbread and a glass of cool,
rich buttermilk; then she came out and sat down beside him.
She began, quite unconsciously, to tell him about herself,—
the things she had done and had not done and the things she
had wished for. She told him of her husband and this new
farm they were trying to buy. She said it was hard to get niggers to work. She said they ought all to be in the chain-gang
and made to work. Even then some ran away. Only yesterday
one had escaped, and another the day before.

At last she gossiped of her neighbors, how good they
were and how bad.

"And do you like them all?" asked the stranger.

She hesitated.

"Most of them," she said; and then, looking up into his face and putting her hand into his, as though he were her father, she said:

"There are none I hate; no, none at all."

He looked away, holding her hand in his, and said dreamily:

"You love your neighbor as yourself?"

She hesitated.

"I try————" she began, and then looked the way he was looking; down under the hill where lay a little, half-ruined cabin.

"They are niggers," she said briefly.

He looked at her. Suddenly a confusion came over her and she insisted, she knew not why.

"But they are niggers!"

With a sudden impulse she arose and hurriedly lighted the lamp that stood just within the door, and held it above her head. She saw his dark face and curly hair. She shrieked in angry terror and rushed down the path, and just as she rushed down, the black convict came running up with hands outstretched. They met in midpath, and before he could stop he had run against her and she fell heavily to earth and lay white and still. Her husband came rushing around the house with a cry and an oath.

"I knew it," he said. "It's that runaway nigger." He held the black man struggling to the earth and raised his voice to a yell. Down the highway came the convict guard, with hound and mob and gun. They paused across the fields. The farmer motioned to them.

"He—attacked—my wife," he gasped.

The mob snarled and worked silently. Right to the limb of the red oak they hoisted the struggling, writhing black man, while others lifted the dazed woman. Right and left, as she tottered to the house, she searched for the stranger with a yearning, but the stranger was gone. And she told none of her guests.

"No—no, I want nothing," she insisted, until they left her, as they thought, asleep. For a time she lay still, listening to the departure of the mob. Then she rose. She shuddered as she heard the creaking of the limb where the body hung. But resolutely she crawled to the window and peered out into the moonlight; she saw the dead man writhe. He stretched his arms out like a cross, looking upward. She gasped and clung to the window sill. Behind the swaying body, and down where the little, half-ruined cabin lay, a single flame flashed up amid the far-off shout and cry of the mob. A fierce joy sobbed up through the terror in her soul and then sank abashed as she watched the flame rise. Suddenly whirling into one great crimson column it shot to the top of the sky and threw great arms athwart the gloom until above the world and behind the roped and swaying form below hung quivering and burning a great crimson cross.

She hid her dizzy, aching head in an agony of tears, and dared not look, for she knew. Her dry lips moved:

"Despised and rejected of men."

She knew, and the very horror of it lifted her dull and shrinking eyelids. There, heaven-tall, earth-wide, hung the stranger on the crimson cross, riven and bloodstained, with thorn-crowned head and pierced hands. She stretched her arms and shrieked.

He did not hear. He did not see. His calm dark eyes, all sorrowful, were fastened on the writhing, twisting body of the thief, and a voice came out of the winds of the night, saying:

"This day thou shalt be with me in Paradise!"

VI | OF THE RULING OF MEN

THE ruling of men is the effort to direct the individual actions of many persons toward some end. This end theoretically should be the greatest good of all, but no human group has ever reached this ideal because of ignorance and selfishness. The simplest object would be rule for the Pleasure of One, namely the Ruler; or of the Few—his favorites; or of many—the Rich, the Privileged, the Powerful. Democratic movements inside groups and nations are always taking place and they are the efforts to increase the number of beneficiaries of the ruling. In 18th century Europe, the effort became so broad and sweeping that an attempt was made at universal expression and the philosophy of the movement said that if All ruled they would rule for All and thus Universal Good was sought through Universal Suffrage.

The unrealized difficulty of this program lay in the widespread ignorance. The mass of men, even of the more intelligent men, not only knew little about each other but less about the action of men in groups and the technique of industry in general. They could only apply universal suffrage, therefore, to the things they knew or knew partially: they knew personal and menial service, individual crafts- manship, agriculture and barter, taxes or the taking of pri- vate property for public ends and the rent of land. With these matters then they attempted to deal. Under the cry of "Freedom" they greatly relaxed the grip of selfish interests by restricting menial service, securing the right of property in handiwork and regulating public taxes; distributing land ownership and freeing trade and barter.

While they were doing this against stubborn resistance, a whole new organization of work suddenly appeared. The suddenness of this "Industrial Revolution" of the 19th cen- tury was partly fortuitous—in the case of Watt's teakettle— partly a natural development, as in the matter of spinning, but largely the determination of powerful and intelligent individuals to secure the benefits of privileged persons, as in the case of foreign slave trade.

The result was on the one hand a vast and unexampled development of industry. Life and civilization in the late 19th and early 20th century were Industry in its whole con- ception, language, and accomplishment: the object of life was to make goods. Now before this giant aspect of things, the new democracy stood aghast and impotent. It could not rule because it did not understand: an invincible kingdom of trade, business, and commerce ruled the world, and before its threshold stood the Freedom of 18th century philosophy warding the way. Some of the very ones who were freed from the tyranny of the Middle Age became the tyrants of the industrial age.

There came a reaction. Men sneered at "democracy" and politics, and brought forth Fate and Philanthropy to rule the world—Fate which gave divine right to rule to the Captains of Industry and their created Millionaires; Philanthropy which organized vast schemes of relief to stop at least the flow of blood in the vaster wounds which industry was making.

It was at this time that the lowest laborers, who worked hardest, got least and suffered most, began to mutter and rebel, and among these were the American Negroes. Lions have no historians, and therefore lion hunts are thrilling and satisfactory human reading. Negroes had no bards, and therefore it has been widely told how American philanthropy freed the slave. In truth the Negro revolted by armed rebellion, by sullen refusal to work, by poison and murder, by running away to the North and Canada, by giving point and powerful example to the agitation of the abolitionists and by furnishing 200,000 soldiers and many times as many civilian helpers in the Civil War. This war was not a war for Negro freedom, but a duel between two industrial systems, one of which was bound to fail because it was an anachronism, and the other bound to succeed because of the Industrial Revolution.

When now the Negro was freed the Philanthropists sought to apply to his situation the Philosophy of Democracy handed down from the 18th century.

There was a chance here to try democratic rule in a new way, that is, against the new industrial oppression with a mass of workers who were not yet in its control. With plenty of land widely distributed, staple products like cotton, rice, and sugar cane, and a thorough system of education, there was a unique chance to realize a new modern democracy in industry in the southern United States which would point the way to the world. This, too, if done by black folk, would have tended to a new unity of human beings and an obliteration of human hatreds festering along the color line.

Efforts were begun. The 14th and 15th amendments gave the right to vote to white and black laborers, and they immediately established a public school system and began to attack the land question. The United States government was seriously considering the distribution of land and capital— "40 acres and a mule"—and the price of cotton opened an easy way to economic independence. Co-operative movements began on a large scale.

But alas! Not only were the former slave-owners solidly arrayed against this experiment, but the owners of the industrial North saw disaster in any such beginnings of industrial democracy. The opposition based its objections on the color line, and Reconstruction became in history a great movement for the self-assertion of the white race against the impudent ambition of degraded blacks, instead of, in truth, the rise of a mass of black and white laborers.

The result was the disfranchisement of the blacks of the South and a world-wide attempt to restrict democratic development to white races and to distract them with race hatred against the darker races. This program, however, although it undoubtedly helped raise the scale of white labor, in much greater proportion put wealth and power in the hands of the great European Captains of Industry and made modern industrial imperialism possible.

This led to renewed efforts on the part of white European workers to understand and apply their political power to its reform through democratic control.

Whether known as Communism or Socialism or what not, these efforts are neither new nor strange nor terrible, but world-old and seeking an absolutely justifiable human ideal—the only ideal that can be sought: the direction of individual action in industry so as to secure the greatest good of all. Marxism was one method of accomplishing this, and its panacea was the doing away with private property in machines and materials. Two mighty attacks were made on this proposal. One was an attack on the fundamental democratic foundation: modern European white industry does not even theoretically seek the good of all, but simply of all Europeans. This attack was virtually unanswered—indeed some Socialists openly excluded Negroes and Asiatics from their scheme. From this it was easy to drift into that form of syndicalism which asks socialism for the skilled laborer only and leaves the common laborer in his bonds.

This throws us back on fundamentals. It compels us again to examine the roots of democracy.

Who may be excluded from a share in the ruling of men? Time and time again the world has answered:

> The Ignorant
> The Inexperienced
> The Guarded
> The Unwilling

That is, we have assumed that only the intelligent should vote, or those who know how to rule men, or those who are not under benevolent guardianship, or those who ardently desire the right.

These restrictions are not arguments for the wide distribution of the ballot—they are rather reasons for restriction addressed to the self-interest of the present real rulers. We say easily, for instance, "The ignorant ought not to vote." We would say, "No civilized state should have citizens too ignorant to participate in government," and this statement is but a step to the fact: that no state is civilized which has citizens too ignorant to help rule it. Or, in other words, education is not a prerequisite to political control—political control is the cause of popular education.

Again, to make experience a qualification for the franchise is absurd: it would stop the spread of democracy and make political power hereditary, a prerequisite of a class, caste, race, or sex. It has of course been soberly argued that only white folk or Englishmen, or men, are really capable of exercising sovereign power in a modern state. The statement proves too much: only yesterday it was Englishmen of high descent, or men of "blood," or sovereigns "by divine right" who could rule. Today the civilized world is being ruled by the descendants of persons who a century ago were pronounced incapable of ever developing a self-ruling people. In every modern state there must come to the polls every generation, and indeed every year, men who are inexperienced in the solutions of the political problems that confront them and who must experiment in methods of ruling men. Thus and thus only will civilization grow.

Again, what is this theory of benevolent guardianship for women, for the masses, for Negroes—for "lesser breeds without the law"? It is simply the old cry of privilege, the old assumption that there are those in the world who know better what is best for others than those others know themselves, and who can be trusted to do this best.

In fact no one knows himself but that self's own soul. The vast and wonderful knowledge of this marvelous universe is locked in the bosoms of its individual souls. To tap this mighty reservoir of experience, knowledge, beauty, love, and deed we must appeal not to the few, not to some souls, but to all. The narrower the appeal, the poorer the culture; the wider the appeal the more magnificent are the possibilities. Infinite is human nature. We make it finite by choking back the mass of men, by attempting to speak for others, to interpret and act for them, and we end by acting for ourselves and using the world as our private property. If this were all, it were crime enough—but it is not all: by our ignorance we make the creation of the greater world impossible; we beat back a world built of the playing of dogs and laughter of children, the song of Black Folk and worship of Yellow, the love of women and strength of men, and try to express by a group of doddering ancients the Will of the World.

There are people who insist upon regarding the franchise, not as a necessity for the many, but as a privilege for the few. They say of persons and classes: "They do not need the ballot." This is often said of women. It is argued that everything which women with the ballot might do for themselves can be done for them; that they have influence and friends "at court," and that their enfranchisement would simply double the number of ballots. So, too, we are told that American Negroes can have done for them by other voters all that they could possibly do for themselves with the ballot and much more because the white voters are more intelligent.

Further than this, it is argued that many of the disfranchised people recognize these facts. "Women do not want the ballot" has been a very effective counter war-cry, so much so that many men have taken refuge in the declaration: "When they want to vote, why, then——" So, too, we are continually told that the "best" Negroes stay out of politics.

Such arguments show so curious a misapprehension of the foundation of the argument for democracy that the argument must be continually restated and emphasized. We must remember that if the theory of democracy is correct, the right to vote is not merely a privilege, not simply a method of meeting the needs of a particular group, and least of all a matter of recognized want or desire. Democracy is a method of realizing the broadest measure of justice to all human beings. The world has, in the past, attempted various methods of attaining this end, most of which can be summed up in three categories:

> The method of the benevolent tyrant.
> The method of the select few.
> The method of the excluded groups.

The method of intrusting the government of a people to a strong ruler has great advantages when the ruler combines strength with ability, unselfish devotion to the public good, and knowledge of what that good calls for. Such a combination is, however, rare and the selection of the right ruler is very difficult. To leave the selection to force is to put a premium on physical strength, chance, and intrigue; to make the selection a matter of birth simply transfers the real power from sovereign to minister. Inevitably the choice of rulers must fall on electors.

Then comes the problem, who shall elect. The earlier answer was: a select few, such as the wise, the best born, the able. Many people assume that it was corruption that made such aristocracies fail. By no means. The best and most effective aristocracy, like the best monarchy, suffered from lack of knowledge. The rulers did not know or understand the needs of the people and they could not find out, for in the last analysis only the man himself, however humble, knows his own condition. He may not know how to remedy it, he may not realize just what is the matter; but he knows when something hurts and he alone knows how that hurt feels. Or if sunk below feeling or comprehension or complaint, he does not even know that he is hurt, God help his country, for it not only lacks knowledge, but has destroyed the sources of knowledge.

So soon as a nation discovers that it holds in the heads and hearts of its individual citizens the vast mine of knowledge, out of which it may build a just government, then more and more it calls those citizens to select their rulers and to judge the justice of their acts.

Even here, however, the temptation is to ask only for the wisdom of citizens of a certain grade or those of recognized worth. Continually some classes are tacitly or expressly excluded. Thus women have been excluded from modern democracy because of the persistent theory of female subjection and because it was argued that their husbands or other male folks would look to their interests. Now, manifestly, most husbands, fathers, and brothers, will, so far as they know how or as they realize women's needs, look after them. But remember the foundation of the argument,—that in the last analysis only the sufferer knows his sufferings and that no state can be strong which excludes from its expressed wisdom the knowledge possessed by mothers, wives, and daughters. We have but to view the unsatisfactory relations of the sexes the world over and the problem of children to realize how desperately we need this excluded wisdom.

The same arguments apply to other excluded groups: if a race, like the Negro race, is excluded, then so far as that race is a part of the economic and social organization of the land, the feeling and the experience of that race are absolutely necessary to the realization of the broadest justice for all citizens. Or if the "submerged tenth" be excluded, then again, there is lost from the world an experience of untold value, and they must be raised rapidly to a place where they can speak for themselves. In the same way and for the same reason children must be educated, insanity prevented, and only those put under the guardianship of others who can in no way be trained to speak for themselves.

The real argument for democracy is, then, that in the people we have the source of that endless life and unbounded wisdom which the rulers of men must have. A given people today may not be intelligent, but through a democratic government that recognizes, not only the worth of the individual to himself, but the worth of his feelings and experiences to all, they can educate, not only the individual unit, but generation after generation, until they accumulate vast stores of wisdom. Democracy alone is the method of showing the whole experience of the race for the benefit of the future and if democracy tries to exclude women or Negroes or the poor or any class because of innate characteristics which do not interfere with intelligence, then that democracy cripples itself and belies its name.

From this point of view we can easily see the weakness and strength of current criticism of extension of the ballot. It is the business of a modern government to see to it, first, that the number of ignorant within its bounds is reduced to the very smallest number. Again, it is the duty of every such government to extend as quickly as possible the number of persons of mature age who can vote. Such possible voters must be regarded, not as sharers of a limited treasure, but as sources of new national wisdom and strength.

The addition of the new wisdom, the new points of view, and the new interests must, of course, be from time to time bewildering and confusing. Today those who have a voice in the body politic have expressed their wishes and sufferings. The result has been a smaller or greater balancing of their conflicting interests. The appearance of new interests and complaints means disarrangement and confusion to the older equilibrium. It is, of course, the inevitable preliminary step to that larger equilibrium in which the interests of no human soul will be neglected. These interests will not, surely, be all fully realized, but they will be recognized and given as full weight as the conflicting interests will allow. The problem of government thereafter would be to reduce the necessary conflict of human interests to the minimum.

From such a point of view one easily sees the strength of the demand for the ballot on the part of certain disfranchised classes. When women ask for the ballot, they are asking, not for a privilege, but for a necessity. You may not see the necessity, you may easily argue that women do not need to vote. Indeed, the women themselves in considerable numbers may agree with you. Nevertheless, women do need the ballot. They need it to right the balance of a world sadly awry because of its brutal neglect of the rights of women and children. With the best will and knowledge, no man can know women's wants as well as women themselves. To disfranchise women is deliberately to turn from knowledge and grope in ignorance.

So, too, with American Negroes: the South continually insists that a benevolent guardianship of whites over blacks is the ideal thing. They assume, that white people not only know better what Negroes need than Negroes themselves, but that they are anxious to supply these needs. As a result they grope in ignorance and helplessness. They cannot "understand" the Negro; they cannot protect him from cheating and lynching; and, in general, instead of loving guardianship we see anarchy and exploitation. If the Negro could speak for himself in the South instead of being spoken for, if he could defend himself instead of having to depend on the chance sympathy of white citizens, how much healthier a growth of democracy the South would have.

So, too, with the darker races of the world. No federation of the world, no true inter-nation—can exclude the black and brown and yellow races from its counsels. They

must equally and according to number act and be heard at
the world's council.

It is not, for a moment, to be assumed that enfranchising
women will not cost something. It will for many years con-
fuse our politics. It may even change the present status of
family life. It will admit to the ballot thousands of inexperienced persons, unable to vote intelligently. Above all, it will
interfere with some of the present prerogatives of men and
probably for some time to come annoy them considerably.

So, too, Negro enfranchisement meant reconstruction,
with its theft and bribery and incompetency as well as its
public schools and enlightened, social legislation. It would
mean today that black men in the South would have to be
treated with consideration, have their wishes respected and
their manhood rights recognized. Every white Southerner,
who wants peons beneath him, who believes in hereditary
menials and a privileged aristocracy, or who hates certain
races because of their characteristics, would resent this.

Notwithstanding this, if America is ever to become a
government built on the broadest justice to every citizen,
then every citizen must be enfranchised. There may be temporary exclusions, until the ignorant and their children are
taught, or to avoid too sudden an influx of inexperienced
voters. But such exclusions can be but temporary if justice
is to prevail.

The principle of basing all government on the consent
of the governed is undenied and undeniable. Moreover, the
method of modern democracy has placed within reach of
the modern state larger reserves of efficiency, ability, and
even genius than the ancient or mediaeval state dreamed of.
That this great work of the past can be carried further
among all races and nations no one can reasonably doubt.

Great as are our human differences and capabilities there

is not the slightest scientific reason for assuming that a given human being of any race or sex cannot reach normal, human development if he is granted a reasonable chance. This is, of course, denied. It is denied so volubly and so frequently and with such positive conviction that the majority of unthinking people seem to assume that most human beings are not human and have no right to human treatment or human opportunity. All this goes to prove that human beings are, and must be, woefully ignorant of each other. It always startles us to find folks thinking like ourselves. We do not really associate with each other, we associate with our ideas of each other, and few people have either the ability or courage to question their own ideas. None have more persistently and dogmatically insisted upon the inherent inferiority of women than the men with whom they come in closest contact. It is the husbands, brothers, and sons of women whom it has been most difficult to induce to consider women seriously or to acknowledge that women have rights which men are bound to respect. So, too, it is those people who live in closest contact with black folk who have most unhesitatingly asserted the utter impossibility of living beside Negroes who are not industrial or political slaves or social pariahs. All this proves that none are so blind as those nearest the thing seen, while, on the other hand, the history of the world is the history of the discovery of the common humanity of human beings among steadily-increasing circles of men.

If the foundations of democracy are thus seen to be sound, how are we going to make democracy effective where it now fails to function—particularly in industry? The Marxists assert that industrial democracy will automatically follow public ownership of machines and materials. Their opponents object that nationalization of machines and materials would not suffice because the mass of people do not understand the industrial process. They do not know:

> What to do
> How to do it
> Who could do it best
>   or
> How to apportion the resulting goods.

There can be no doubt but that monopoly of machines and materials is a chief source of the power of industrial tyrants over the common worker and that monopoly today is due as much to chance, and cheating as to thrift and intelligence. So far as it is due to chance and cheating, the argument for public ownership of capital is incontrovertible even though it involves some interference with long vested rights and inheritance. This is being widely recognized in the whole civilized world. But how about the accumulation of goods due to thrift and intelligence—would democracy in industry interfere here to such an extent as to discourage enterprise and make impossible the intelligent direction of the mighty and intricate industrial process of modern times?

The knowledge of what to do in industry and how to do it in order to attain the resulting goods rests in the hands and brains of the workers and managers, and the judges of the result are the public. Consequently it is not so much a question as to whether the world will admit democratic control here as how can such control be long avoided when the people once understand the fundamentals of industry. How can civilization persist in letting one person or a group of persons, by secret inherent power, determine what goods shall be made—whether bread or champagne, overcoats or silk socks? Can so vast a power be kept from the people?

But it may be opportunely asked: has our experience in electing public officials led us to think that we could run railways, cotton mills, and department stores by popular vote? The answer is clear: no, it has not, and the reason has been lack of interest in politics and the tyranny of the Majority. Politics have not touched the matters of daily life which are nearest the interests of the people—namely, work and wages; or if they have, they have touched it obscurely and indirectly. When voting touches the vital, everyday interests of all, nominations and elections will call for more intelligent activity. Consider too the vast unused and misused power of public rewards to obtain ability and genius for the service of the state. If millionaires can buy science and art, cannot the Democratic state outbid them not only with money but with the vast ideal of the common weal?

There still remains, however, the problem of the Majority.

What is the cause of the undoubted reaction and alarm that the citizens of democracy continually feel? It is, I am sure, the failure to feel the full significance of the change of rule from a privileged minority to that of an omnipotent majority, and the assumption that mere majority rule is the last word of government; that majorities have no responsibilities, that they rule by the grace of God. Granted that government should be based on the consent of the governed, does the consent of a majority at any particular time adequately express the consent of all? Has the minority, even though a small and unpopular and unfashionable minority, no right to respectful consideration?

I remember that excellent little high school text book, "Nordhoff's Politics," where I first read of government, saying this sentence at the beginning of its most important chapter: "The first duty of a minority is to become a majority." This is a statement which has its underlying truth, but it also has its dangerous falsehood; viz., any minority which cannot become a majority is not worthy of any consideration. But suppose that the out-voted minority is necessarily always a minority? Women, for instance, can seldom expect to be a majority; artists must always be the few; ability is always rare, and black folk in this land are but a tenth. Yet to tyrannize over such minorities, to browbeat and insult them, to call that government a democracy which makes majority votes an excuse for crushing ideas and individuality and self-development, is manifestly a peculiarly dangerous perversion of the real democratic ideal. It is right here, in its method and not in its object, that democracy in America and elsewhere has so often failed. We have attempted to enthrone any chance majority and make it rule by divine right. We have kicked and cursed minorities as upstarts and usurpers when their sole offense lay in not having ideas or hair like ours. Efficiency, ability, and genius found often no abiding place in such a soil as this. Small wonder that revolt has come and high-handed methods are rife, of pretending that policies which we favor or persons that we like have the anointment of a purely imaginary majority vote.

Are the methods of such a revolt wise, howsoever great the provocation and evil may be? If the absolute monarchy of majorities is galling and inefficient, is it any more inefficient than the absolute monarchy of individuals or privileged classes have been found to be in the past? Is the appeal from a numerous-minded despot to a smaller, privileged group or to one man likely to remedy matters permanently? Shall we step backward a thousand years because our present problem is baffling?

Surely not and surely, too, the remedy for absolutism lies

in calling these same minorities to council. As the king-in-council succeeded the king by the grace of God, so in future democracies the toleration and encouragement of minorities and the willingness to consider as " men" the crankiest, humblest and poorest and blackest peoples, must be the real key to the consent of the governed. Peoples and governments will not in the future assume that because they have the brute power to enforce momentarily dominant ideas, it is best to do so without thoughtful conference with the ideas of smaller groups and individuals. Proportionate representation in physical and spiritual form must come.

That this method is virtually coming in vogue we can see by the minority groups of modern legislatures. Instead of the artificial attempts to divide all possible ideas and plans between two great parties, modern legislatures in advanced nations tend to develop smaller and smaller minority groups, while government is carried on by temporary coalitions. For a time we inveighed against this and sought to consider it a perversion of the only possible method of practical democracy. Today we are gradually coming to realize that government by temporary coalition of small and diverse groups may easily become the most efficient method of expressing the will of man and of setting the human soul free. The only hindrance to the faster development of this government by allied minorities is the fear of external war which is used again and again to melt these living, human, thinking groups into inhuman, thoughtless, and murdering machines.

The persons, then, who come forward in the dawn of the 20th century to help in the ruling of men must come with the firm conviction that no nation, race, or sex, has a monopoly of ability or ideas; that no human group is so small as to deserve to be ignored as a part, and as an integral and respected part, of the mass of men; that, above all, no

group of twelve million black folk, even though they are at
the physical mercy of a hundred million white majority, can
be deprived of a voice in their government and of the right
to self-development without a blow at the very foundations
of all democracy and all human uplift; that the very criticism aimed today at universal suffrage is in reality a demand
for power on the part of consciously efficient minorities,—
but these minorities face a fatal blunder when they assume
that less democracy will give them and their kind greater
efficiency. However desperate the temptation, no modern
nation can shut the gates of opportunity in the face of its
women, its peasants, its laborers, or its socially damned.
How astounded the future world-citizen will be to know
that as late as 1918 great and civilized nations were making
desperate endeavor to confine the development of ability
and individuality to one sex,—that is, to one-half of the
nation; and he will probably learn that similar effort to confine humanity to one race lasted a hundred years longer.

The doctrine of the divine right of majorities leads to
almost humorous insistence on a dead level of mediocrity.
It demands that all people be alike or that they be ostracized.
At the same time its greatest accusation against rebels is this
same desire to be alike: the suffragette is accused of wanting
to be a man, the socialist is accused of envy of the rich, and
the black man is accused of wanting to be white. That any
one of these should simply want to be himself is to the
average worshiper of the majority inconceivable, and yet of
all worlds, may the good Lord deliver us from a world
where everybody looks like his neighbor and thinks like his
neighbor and is like his neighbor.

The world has long since awakened to a realization of
the evil which a privileged few may exercise over the
majority of a nation. So vividly has this truth been brought

home to us that we have lightly assumed that a privileged and enfranchised majority cannot equally harm a nation. Insane, wicked, and wasteful as the tyranny of the few over the many may be, it is not more dangerous than the tyranny of the many over the few. Brutal physical revolution can, and usually does, end the tyranny of the few. But the spiritual losses from suppressed minorities may be vast and fatal and yet all unknown and unrealized because idea and dream and ability are paralyzed by brute force.

If, now, we have a democracy with no excluded groups, with all men and women enfranchised, what is such a democracy to do? How will it function? What will be its field of work?

The paradox which faces the civilized world today is that democratic control is everywhere limited in its control of human interests. Mankind is engaged in planting, forestry, and mining, preparing food and shelter, making clothes and machines, transporting goods and folk, disseminating news, distributing products, doing public and private personal service, teaching, advancing science, and creating art.

In this intricate whirl of activities, the theory of government has been hitherto to lay down only very general rules of conduct, marking the limits of extreme anti-social acts, like fraud, theft, and murder.

The theory was that within these bounds was Freedom —the Liberty to think and do and move as one wished. The real realm of freedom was found in experience to be much narrower than this in one direction and much broader in another. In matters of Truth and Faith and Beauty, the Ancient Law was inexcusably strait and modern law unforgivably stupid. It is here that the future and mighty fight for Freedom must and will be made. Here in the heavens and on the mountaintops, the air of Freedom is wide, almost limitless, for here, in the highest stretches, individual freedom harms no man, and, therefore, no man has the right to limit it.

On the other hand, in the valleys of the hard, unyielding laws of matter and the social necessities of time production, and human intercourse, the limits on our freedom are stern and unbending if we would exist and thrive. This does not say that everything here is governed by incontrovertible "natural" law which needs no human decision as to raw materials, machinery, prices, wages, news-dissemination, education of children, etc.; but it does mean that decisions here must be limited by brute facts and based on science and human wants.

Today the scientific and ethical boundaries of our industrial activities are not in the hands of scientists, teachers, and thinkers; nor is the intervening opportunity for decision left in the control of the public whose welfare such decisions guide. On the contrary, the control of industry is largely in the hands of a powerful few, who decide for their own good and regardless of the good of others. The making of the rules of Industry, then, is not in the hands of All, but in the hands of the Few. The Few who govern industry envisage, not the wants of mankind, but their own wants. They work quietly, often secretly, opposing Law, on the one hand, as interfering with the "freedom of industry"; opposing, on the other hand, free discussion and open determination of the rules of work and wealth and wages, on the ground that harsh natural law brooks no interference by Democracy.

These things today, then, are not matters of free discussion and determination. They are strictly controlled. Who controls them? Who makes these inner, but powerful, rules?

Few people know. Others assert and believe these rules are "natural"—a part of our inescapable physical environment. Some of them doubtless are; but most of them are just as clearly the dictates of self-interest laid down by the powerful private persons who today control industry: Just here it is that modern men demand that Democracy supplant skilfully concealed, but all too evident, Monarchy.

In industry, monarchy and the aristocracy rule, and there are those who, calling themselves democratic, believe that democracy can never enter here. Industry, they maintain, is a matter of technical knowledge and ability, and, therefore, is the eternal heritage of the few. They point to the failure of attempts at democratic control in industry, just as we used to point to Spanish-American governments, and they expose, not simply the failures of Russian Soviets,—they fly to arms to prevent that greatest experiment in industrial democracy which the world has yet seen. These are the ones who say: We must control labor or civilization will fail; we must control white labor in Europe and America; above all, we must control yellow labor in Asia and black labor in Africa and the South, else we shall have no tea, or rubber, or cotton. And yet,—and yet is it so easy to give up the dream of democracy? Must industry rule men or may men rule even industry? And unless men rule industry, can they ever hope really to make laws or educate children or create beauty?

That the problem of the democratization of industry is tremendous, let no man deny. We must spread that sympathy and intelligence which tolerates the widest individual freedom despite the necessary public control; we must learn to select for public office ability rather than mere affability. We must stand ready to defer to knowledge and science and judge by result rather than by method; and finally we must face the fact that the final distribution of goods—the question of wages and income is an ethical and not a mere mechanical problem and calls for grave public human judgment and not secrecy and closed doors. All this means time and development. It comes not complete by instant revolution of a day, nor yet by the deferred evolution of a thousand years—it comes daily, bit by bit and step by step, as men and women learn and grow and as children are trained in Truth.

These steps are in many cases clear: the careful, steady increase of public democratic ownership of industry, beginning with the simplest type of public utilities and monopolies, and extending gradually as we learn the way; the use of taxation to limit inheritance and to take the unearned increment for public use beginning (but not ending) with a "single tax" on monopolized land values; the training of the public in business technique by co-operation in buying and selling, and in industrial technique by the shop committee and manufacturing guild.

But beyond all this must come the Spirit—the Will to Human Brotherhood of all Colors, Races, and Creeds; the Wanting of the Wants of All. Perhaps the finest contribution of current Socialism to the world is neither its light nor its dogma, but the idea back of its one mighty word—Comrade!

The Call

In the Land of the Heavy Laden came once a dreary day. And the King, who sat upon the Great White Throne, raised his eyes and saw afar off how the hills around were hot with hostile feet and the sound of the mocking of his enemies struck anxiously on the King's ears, for the King loved his enemies. So the King lifted up his hand in the glittering silence and spake softly, saying: "Call the Servants of the King." Then the herald stepped before the armpost of the throne, and cried: "Thus saith the High and Mighty One, who inhabiteth Eternity, whose name is Holy,—the Servants of the King!"

Now, of the servants of the king there were a hundred and forty-four thousand,—tried men and brave, brawny of arm and quick of wit; aye, too, and women of wisdom and women marvelous in beauty and grace. And yet on this drear day when the King called, their ears were thick with the dust of the enemy, their eyes were blinded with the flashing of his spears, and they hid their faces in dread silence and moved not, even at the King's behest. So the herald called again. And the servants cowered in very shame, but none came forth. But the third blast of the herald struck upon a woman's heart, afar. And the woman straightway left her baking and sweeping and the rattle of pans; and the woman straightway left her chatting and gossiping and the sewing of garments, and the woman stood before the King, saying: "The servant of thy servants, O Lord."

Then the King smiled,—smiled wondrously, so that the setting sun burst through the clouds, and the hearts of the King's men dried hard within them. And the low-voiced King said, so low that even they that listened heard not well: "Go, smite me mine enemies, that they cease to do evil in my sight." And the woman quailed and trembled. Three times she lifted her eyes unto the hills and saw the heathen whirling onward in their rage. And seeing, she shrank—three times she shrank and crept to the King's feet.

"O King," she cried, "I am but a woman."

And the King answered: "Go, then, Mother of Men."

And the woman said, "Nay, King, but I am still a maid." Whereat the King cried: "O maid, made Man, thou shalt be Bride of God."

And yet the third time the woman shrank at the thunder in her ears, and whispered: "Dear God, I am black!"

The King spake not, but swept the veiling of his face aside and lifted up the light of his countenance upon her and lo! it was black.

So the woman went forth on the hills of God to do battle for the King, on that drear day in the land of the Heavy Laden, when the heathen raged and imagined a vain thing.

VII | THE DAMNATION OF WOMEN

I REMEMBER four women of my boyhood: my mother, cousin Inez, Emma, and Ide Fuller. They represented the problem of the widow, the wife, the maiden, and the outcast. They were, in color, brown and light brown, yellow with brown freckles, and white. They existed not for themselves, but for men; they were named after the men to whom they were related and not after the fashion of their own souls.

They were not beings, they were relations and these relations were enfilmed with mystery and secrecy. We did not know the truth or believe it when we heard it. Motherhood! What was it? We did not know or greatly care. My mother and I were good chums. I liked her. After she was dead I loved her with a fierce sense of personal loss.

Inez was a pretty, brown cousin who married. What was marriage? We did not know, neither did she, poor thing! It came to mean for her a litter of children, poverty, a drunken, cruel companion, sickness, and death. Why?

There was no sweeter sight than Emma,—slim, straight, and dainty, darkly flushed with the passion of youth; but her life was a wild, awful struggle to crush her natural, fierce joy of love. She crushed it and became a cold, calculating mockery.

Last there was that awful outcast of the town, the white woman, Ide Fuller. What she was, we did not know. She stood to us as embodied filth and wrong,—but whose filth, whose wrong?

Grown up I see the problem of these women transfused; I hear all about me the unanswered call of youthful love, none the less glorious because of its clean, honest, physical passion. Why unanswered? Because the youth are too poor to marry or if they marry, too poor to have children. They turn aside, then, in three directions: to marry for support, to what men call shame, or to that which is more evil than nothing. It is an unendurable paradox; it must be changed or the bases of culture will totter and fall.

The world wants healthy babies and intelligent workers. Today we refuse to allow the combination and force thousands of intelligent workers to go childless at a horrible expenditure of moral force, or we damn them if they break our idiotic conventions. Only at the sacrifice of intelligence and the chance to do their best work can the majority of modern women bear children. This is the damnation of women.

All womanhood is hampered today because the world on which it is emerging is a world that tries to worship both virgins and mothers and in the end despises motherhood and despoils virgins.

The future woman must have a life work and economic independence. She must have knowledge. She must have the right of motherhood at her own discretion. The present mincing horror at free womanhood must pass if we are ever to be rid of the bestiality of free manhood; not by guarding the weak in weakness do we gain strength, but by making weakness free and strong.

The world must choose the free woman or the white wraith of the prostitute. Today it wavers between the prostitute and the nun. Civilization must show two things: the glory and beauty of creating life and the need and duty of power and intelligence. This and this only will make the perfect marriage of love and work.

> God is Love,
> Love is God;
> There is no God but Love
> And Work is His Prophet!

All this of woman,—but what of black women?

The world that wills to worship womankind studiously forgets its darker sisters. They seem in a sense to typify that veiled Melancholy:

> "Whose saintly visage is too bright
> To hit the sense of human sight,
> And, therefore, to our weaker view
> O'er-laid with black."

Yet the world must heed these daughters of sorrow, from the primal black All-Mother of men down through the ghostly throng of mighty womanhood, who walked in the mysterious dawn of Asia and Africa; from Neith, the primal mother of all, whose feet rest on hell, and whose almighty hands uphold the heavens; all religion, from beauty to beast, lies on her eager breasts; her body bears the stars, while her shoulders are necklaced by the dragon; from black Neith down to

"That starr'd Ethiop queen who strove
To set her beauty's praise above
The sea-nymphs,"

through dusky Cleopatras, dark Candaces, and darker, fiercer Zinghas, to our own day and our own land,—in gentle Phillis; Harriet, the crude Moses; the sybil, Sojourner Truth; and the martyr, Louise De Mortie.

The father and his worship is Asia; Europe is the precocious, self-centered, forward-striving child; but the land of the mother is and was Africa. In subtle and mysterious way, despite her curious history, her slavery, polygamy, and toil, the spell of the African mother pervades her land. Isis, the mother, is still titular goddess, in thought if not in name, of the dark continent. Nor does this all seem to be solely a survival of the historic matriarchate through which all nations pass,—it appears to be more than this,—as if the great black race in passing up the steps of human culture gave the world, not only the Iron Age, the cultivation of the soil, and the domestication of animals, but also, in peculiar emphasis, the mother-idea.

"No mother can love more tenderly and none is more tenderly loved than the Negro mother," writes Schneider. Robin tells of the slave who bought his mother's freedom instead of his own. Mungo Park writes: "Everywhere in Africa, I have noticed that no greater affront can be offered a Negro than insulting his mother. 'Strike me,' cries a Mandingo to his enemy, 'but revile not my mother!' " And the Krus and Fantis say the same. The peoples on the Zambezi and the great lakes cry in sudden fear or joy: "O, my mother!" And the Herero swears (endless oath) "By my mother's tears!" "As the mist in the swamps," cries the Angola Negro, "so lives the love of father and mother."

A student of the present Gold Coast life describes the work of the village headman, and adds: "It is a difficult task that he is set to, but in this matter he has all-powerful helpers in the female members of the family, who will be either the aunts or the sisters or the cousins or the nieces of the headman, and as their interests are identical with his in every particular, the good women spontaneously train up their children to implicit obedience to the headman, whose rule in the family thus becomes a simple and an easy matter. 'The hand that rocks the cradle rules the world.' What a power for good in the native state system would the mothers of the Gold Coast and Ashanti become by judicious training upon native lines!"

Schweinfurth declares of one tribe: "A bond between mother and child which lasts for life is the measure of affection shown among the Dyoor" and Ratzel adds:

"Agreeable to the natural relation the mother stands first among the chief influences affecting the children. From the Zulus to the Waganda, we find the mother the most influential counsellor at the court of ferocious sovereigns, like Chaka or Mtesa; sometimes sisters take her place. Thus even with chiefs who possess wives by hundreds the bonds of blood are the strongest and that the woman, though often heavily burdened, is in herself held in no small esteem among the Negroes is clear from the numerous Negro queens, from the medicine women, from the participation in public meetings permitted to women by many Negro peoples."

As I remember through memories of others, backward among my own family, it is the mother I ever recall,—the little, far-off mother of my grandmothers, who sobbed her life away in song, longing for her lost palm-trees and scented waters; the tall and bronzen grandmother, with beaked nose and shrewish eyes, who loved and scolded her black and laughing husband as he smoked lazily in his high oak chair; above all, my own mother, with all her soft brownness, the brown velvet of her skin, the sorrowful black-brown of her eyes, and the tiny brown-capped waves of her midnight hair as it lay new parted on her forehead. All the way back in these dim distances it is mothers and mothers of mothers who seem to count, while fathers are shadowy memories.

Upon this African mother-idea, the westward slave trade and American slavery struck like doom. In the cruel exigencies of the traffic in men and in the sudden, unprepared emancipation the great pendulum of social equilibrium swung from a time, in 1800,—when America had but eight or less black women to every ten black men,—all too swiftly to a day, in 1870,—when there were nearly eleven women to ten men in our Negro population. This was but the outward numerical fact of social dislocation; within lay polygamy, polyandry, concubinage, and moral degradation, They fought against all this desperately, did these black slaves in the West Indies, especially among the half-free artisans; they set up their ancient household gods, and when Toussaint and Cristophe founded their kingdom in Haiti, it was based on old African tribal ties and beneath it was the mother-idea.

The crushing weight of slavery fell on black women. Under it there was no legal marriage, no legal family, no legal control over children. To be sure, custom and religion replaced here and there what the law denied, yet one has but to read advertisements like the following to see the hell beneath the system:

"One hundred dollars reward will be given for my two fellows, Abram and Frank. Abram has a wife at Colonel

Stewart's, in Liberty County, and a mother at Thunderbolt, and a sister in Savannah.

"WILLIAM ROBERTS."

"Fifty dollars reward—Ran away from the subscriber a Negro girl named Maria. She is of a copper color, between thirteen and fourteen years of age—bareheaded and barefooted. She is small for her age—very sprightly and very likely. She stated she was going to see her mother at Maysville.

"SANFORD THOMSON."

"Fifty dollars reward—Ran away from the subscriber his Negro man Pauladore, commonly called Paul. I understand General R. Y. Hayne has purchased his wife and children from H. L. Pinckney, Esq., and has them now on his plantation at Goose Creek, where, no doubt, the fellow is frequently lurking.

"T. DAVIS."

The Presbyterian synod of Kentucky said to the churches under its care in 1835: "Brothers and sisters, parents and children, husbands and wives, are torn asunder and permitted to see each other no more. These acts are daily occurring in the midst of us. The shrieks and agony often witnessed on such occasions proclaim, with a trumpet tongue, the iniquity of our system. There is not a neighborhood where these heartrending scenes are not displayed. There is not a village or road that does not behold the sad procession of manacled outcasts whose mournful countenances tell that they are exiled by force from all that their hearts hold dear."

A sister of a president of the United States declared:

"We Southern ladies are complimented with the names of wives, but we are only the mistresses of seraglios."

Out of this, what sort of black women could be born into the world of today? There are those who hasten to answer this query in scathing terms and who say lightly and repeatedly that out of black slavery came nothing decent in womanhood; that adultery and uncleanness were their heritage and are their continued portion.

Fortunately so exaggerated a charge is humanly impossible of truth. The half-million women of Negro descent who lived at the beginning of the 19th century had become the mothers of two and one-fourth million daughters at the time of the Civil War and five million granddaughters in 1910. Can all these women be vile and the hunted race continue to grow in wealth and character? Impossible. Yet to save from the past the shreds and vestiges of self-respect has been a terrible task. I most sincerely doubt if any other race of women could have brought its fineness up through so devilish a fire.

Alexander Crummell once said of his sister in the blood: "In her girlhood all the delicate tenderness of her sex has been rudely outraged. In the field, in the rude cabin, in the press-room, in the factory she was thrown into the companionship of coarse and ignorant men. No chance was given her for delicate reserve or tender modesty. From her childhood she was the doomed victim of the grossest passion. All the virtues of her sex were utterly ignored. If the instinct of chastity asserted itself, then she had to fight like a tiger for the ownership and possession of her own person and ofttimes had to suffer pain and lacerations for her virtuous self-assertion. When she reached maturity, all the tender instincts of her womanhood were ruthlessly violated. At the age of marriage,—always prematurely anticipated under slavery—she was mated as the stock of the plantation were mated, not to be the companion of a loved and chosen husband, but to be the breeder of human cattle for the field or the auction block."

Down in such mire has the black motherhood of this race struggled,—starving its own wailing offspring to nurse to the world their swaggering masters; welding for its children chains which affronted even the moral sense of an unmoral world. Many a man and woman in the South have lived in wedlock as holy as Adam and Eve and brought forth their brown and golden children, but because the darker woman was helpless, her chivalrous and whiter mate could cast her off at his pleasure and publicly sneer at the body he had privately blasphemed.

I shall forgive the white South much in its final judgment day: I shall forgive its slavery, for slavery is a world-old habit; I shall forgive its fighting for a well-lost cause, and for remembering that struggle with tender tears; I shall forgive its so-called "pride of race," the passion of its hot blood, and even its dear, old, laughable strutting and posing; but one thing I shall never forgive, neither in this world nor the world to come: its wanton and continued and persistent insulting of the black womanhood which it sought and seeks to prostitute to its lust. I cannot forget that it is such Southern gentlemen into whose hands smug Northern hypocrites of today are seeking to place our women's eternal destiny,—men who insist upon withholding from my mother and wife and daughter those signs and appellations of courtesy and respect which elsewhere he withholds only from bawds and courtesans.

The result of this history of insult and degradation has been both fearful and glorious. It has birthed the haunting prostitute, the brawler, and the beast of burden; but, it has also given the world an efficient womanhood, whose strength lies in its freedom and whose chastity was won in the teeth of temptation and not in prison and swaddling clothes.

To no modern race does its women mean so much as to the Negro nor come so near to the fulfilment of its meaning. As one of our women writes: "Only the black woman can say 'when and where I enter, in the quiet, undisputed dignity of my womanhood, without violence and without suing or special patronage, then and there the whole Negro race enters with me.' "

They came first, in earlier days, like foam flashing on dark, silent waters,—bits of stern, dark womanhood here and there tossed almost carelessly aloft to the world's notice. First and naturally they assumed the panoply of the ancient African mother of men, strong and black, whose very nature beat back the wilderness of oppression and contempt. Such a one was that cousin of my grandmother, whom western Massachusetts remembers as "Mum Bett." Scarred for life by a blow received in defense of a sister, she ran away to Great Barrington and was the first slave, or one of the first, to be declared free under the Bill of Rights of 1780. The son of the judge who freed her, writes:

"Even in her humble station, she had, when occasion required it, an air of command which conferred a degree of dignity and gave her an ascendancy over those of her rank, which is very unusual in persons of any rank or color. Her determined and resolute character, which enabled her to limit the ravages of Shay's mob, was manifested in her conduct and deportment during her whole life. She claimed no distinction, but it was yielded to her from her superior experience, energy, skill, and sagacity. Having known this woman as familiarly as I knew either of my parents, I cannot believe in the moral or physical inferiority of the race to which she belonged. The degradation of the African must have been otherwise caused than by natural inferiority."

It was such strong women that laid the foundations of the great Negro church of today, with its five million members and ninety millions of dollars in property. One of the early mothers of the church, Mary Still, writes thus quaintly, in the forties:

"When we were as castouts and spurned from the large churches, driven from our knees, pointed at by the proud, neglected by the careless, without a place of worship, Allen, faithful to the heavenly calling, came forward and laid the foundation of this connection. The women, like the women at the sepulcher, were early to aid in laying the foundation of the temple and in helping to carry up the noble structure and in the name of their God set up their banner; most of our aged mothers are gone from this to a better state of things. Yet some linger still on their staves, watching with intense interest the ark as it moves over the tempestuous waves of opposition and ignorance. . . .

"But the labors of these women stopped not here, for they knew well that they were subject to affliction and death. For the purpose of mutual aid, they banded themselves together in society capacity, that they might be better able to administer to each others' sufferings and to soften their own pillows. So we find the females in the early history of the church abounding in good works and in acts of true benevolence."

From such spiritual ancestry came two striking figures of war-time,—Harriet Tubman and Sojourner Truth.

For eight or ten years previous to the breaking out of the Civil War, Harriet Tubman was a constant attendant at anti-slavery conventions, lectures, and other meetings; she was a black woman of medium size, smiling countenance, with her upper front teeth gone, attired in coarse but neat clothes, and carrying always an old-fashioned reticule at her side. Usually as soon as she sat down she would drop off in sound sleep.

She was born a slave in Maryland, in 1820, bore the marks of the lash on her flesh; and had been made partially deaf, and perhaps to some degree mentally unbalanced by a blow on the head in childhood. Yet she was one of the most important agents of the Underground Railroad and a leader of fugitive slaves. She ran away in 1849 and went to Boston in 1854, where she was welcomed into the homes of the leading abolitionists and where every one listened with tense interest to her strange stories. She was absolutely illiterate, with no knowledge of geography, and yet year after year she penetrated the slave states and personally led North over three hundred fugitives without losing a single one. A standing reward of $10,000 was offered for her, but as she said: "The whites cannot catch us, for I was born with the charm, and the Lord has given me the power." She was one of John Brown's closest advisers and only severe sickness prevented her presence at Harper's Ferry.

When the war cloud broke, she hastened to the front, flitting down along her own mysterious paths, haunting the armies in the field, and serving as guide and nurse and spy. She followed Sherman in his great march to the sea and was with Grant at Petersburg, and always in the camps the Union officers silently saluted her.

The other woman belonged to a different type, a tall, gaunt, black, unsmiling sybil, weighted with the woe of the world. She ran away from slavery and giving up her own name took the name of Sojourner Truth. She says: "I can remember when I was a little, young girl, how my old mammy would sit out of doors in the evenings and look up at the stars and groan, and I would say, 'Mammy, what makes you groan so?' And she would say, 'I am groaning to think of my poor children; they do not know where I be and I don't know where they be. I look up at the stars and they look up at the stars!' "

Her determination was founded on unwavering faith in ultimate good. Wendell Phillips says that he was once in Faneuil Hall, when Frederick Douglass was one of the chief speakers. Douglass had been describing the wrongs of the Negro race and as he proceeded he grew more and more excited and finally ended by saying that they had no hope of justice from the whites, no possible hope except in their own right arms. It must come to blood! They must fight for themselves. Sojourner Truth was sitting, tall and dark, on the very front seat facing the platform, and in the hush of feeling when Douglass sat down she spoke out in her deep, peculiar voice, heard all over the hail:

"Frederick, is God dead?"

Such strong, primitive types of Negro womanhood in America seem to some to exhaust its capabilities. They know less of a not more worthy, but a finer type of black woman wherein trembles all of that delicate sense of beauty and striving for self-realization, which is as characteristic of the Negro soul as is its quaint strength and sweet laughter. George Washington wrote in grave and gentle courtesy to a Negro woman, in 1776, that he would "be happy to see" at his headquarters at any time, a person "to whom nature has been so liberal and beneficial in her dispensations." This child, Phillis Wheatley, sang her trite and halting strain to a world that wondered and could not produce her like. Measured today her muse was slight and yet, feeling her striving spirit, we call to her still in her own words: "Through thickest glooms look back, immortal shade."

Perhaps even higher than strength and art loom human sympathy and sacrifice as characteristic of Negro womanhood. Long years ago, before the Declaration of Independence, Kate Ferguson was born in New York. Freed, widowed, and bereaved of her children before she was twenty, she took the children of the streets of New York, white and black, to her empty arms, taught them, found them homes, and with Dr. Mason of Murray Street Church established the first modern Sunday School in Manhattan.

Sixty years later came Mary Shadd up out of Delaware. She was tall and slim, of that ravishing dream-born beauty,—that twilight of the races which we call mulatto. Well-educated, vivacious, with determination shining from her sharp eyes, she threw herself singlehanded into the great Canadian pilgrimage when thousands of hunted black men hurried northward and crept beneath the protection of the lion's paw. She became teacher, editor, and lecturer; tramping afoot through winter snows, pushing without blot or blemish through crowd and turmoil to conventions and meetings, and finally becoming recruiting agent for the United States government in gathering Negro soldiers in the West.

After the war the sacrifice of Negro women for freedom and uplift is one of the finest chapters in their history. Let one life typify all: Louise De Mortie, a free-born Virginia girl, had lived most of her life in Boston. Her high forehead, swelling lips, and dark eyes marked her for a woman of feeling and intellect. She began a successful career as a public reader. Then came the War and the Call. She went to the orphaned colored children of New Orleans,—out of freedom into insult and oppression and into the teeth of the yellow fever. She toiled and dreamed. In 1887 she had raised money and built an orphan home and that same year, in the thirty-fourth of her young life, she died, saying simply: "I belong to God."

As I look about me today in this veiled world of mine, despite the noisier and more spectacular advance of my brothers, I instinctively feel and know that it is the five million women of my race who really count. Black women (and women whose grandmothers were black) are today furnishing our teachers; they are the main pillars of those social settlements which we call churches; and they have with small doubt raised three-fourths of our church property. If we have today, as seems likely, over a billion dollars of accumulated goods, who shall say how much of it has been wrung from the hearts of servant girls and washer-women and women toilers in the fields? As makers of two million homes these women are today seeking in marvelous ways to show forth our strength and beauty and our conception of the truth.

In the United States in 1910 there were 4,931,882 women of Negro descent; over twelve hundred thousand of these were children, another million were girls and young women under twenty, and two and a half-million were adults. As a mass these women were unlettered,—a fourth of those from fifteen to twenty-five years of age were unable to write. These women are passing through, not only a moral, but an economic revolution. Their grandmothers married at twelve and fifteen, but twenty-seven percent of these women today who have passed fifteen are still single.

Yet these black women toil and toil hard. There were in 1910 two and a half million Negro homes in the United States. Out of these homes walked daily to work two million women and girls over ten years of age,—over half of the colored female population as against a fifth in the case of white women. These, then, are a group of workers, fighting for their daily bread like men; independent and approaching economic freedom! They furnished a million farm laborers, 80,000 farmers, 22,000 teachers, 600,000 servants and washerwomen, and 50,000 in trades and merchandizing.

The family group, however, which is the ideal of the culture with which these folk have been born, is not based on the idea of an economically independent working mother. Rather its ideal harks back to the sheltered harem with the mother emerging at first as nurse and homemaker, while the man remains the sole breadwinner. What is the inevitable result of the clash of such ideals and such facts in the colored group? Broken families.

Among native white women one in ten is separated from her husband by death, divorce, or desertion. Among Negroes the ratio is one in seven. Is the cause racial? No, it is economic, because there is the same high ratio among the white foreign-born. The breaking up of the present family is the result of modern working and sex conditions and it hits the laborers with terrible force. The Negroes are put in a peculiarly difficult position, because the wage of the male breadwinner is below the standard, while the openings for colored women in certain lines of domestic work, and now in industries, are many. Thus while toil holds the father and brother in country and town at low wages, the sisters and mothers are called to the city. As a result the Negro women outnumber the men nine or ten to eight in many cities, making what Charlotte Gilman bluntly calls "cheap women."

What shall we say to this new economic equality in a great laboring class? Some people within and without the race deplore it. "Back to the homes with the women," they cry, "and higher wage for the men." But how impossible this is has been shown by war conditions. Cessation of foreign migration has raised Negro men's wages, to be sure—but it has not only raised Negro women's wages, it has opened to them a score of new avenues of earning a living. Indeed, here, in microcosm and with differences emphasizing sex equality, is the industrial history of labor in the 19th and 20th centuries. We cannot abolish the new economic freedom of women. We cannot imprison women again in a home or require them all on pain of death to be nurses and housekeepers.

What is today the message of these black women to America and to the world? The uplift of women is, next to the problem of the color line and the peace movement, our greatest modern cause. When, now, two of these movements—woman and color—combine in one, the combination has deep meaning.

In other years women's way was clear: to be beautiful, to be petted, to bear children. Such has been their theoretic destiny and if perchance they have been ugly, hurt, and barren, that has been forgotten with studied silence. In partial compensation for this narrowed destiny the white world has lavished its politeness on its womankind,—its chivalry and bows, its uncoverings and courtesies—all the accumulated homage disused for courts and kings and craving exercise. The revolt of white women against this preordained destiny has in these latter days reached splendid proportions, but it is the revolt of an aristocracy of brains and ability,—the middle class and rank and file still plod on in the appointed path, paid by the homage, the almost mocking homage, of men.

From black women of America, however, (and from some others, too, but chiefly from black women and their daughters' daughters) this gauze has been withheld and without semblance of such apology they have been frankly trodden under the feet of men. They are and have been objected to, apparently for reasons peculiarly exasperating to reasoning human beings. When in this world a man comes forward with a thought, a deed, a vision, we ask not, how does he look,—but what is his message? It is of but passing interest whether or not the messenger is beautiful or ugly,— the message is the thing. This, which is axiomatic among men, has been in past ages but partially true if the messenger was a woman. The world still wants to ask that a woman primarily be pretty and if she is not, the mob pouts and asks querulously, "What else are women for?" Beauty "is its own excuse for being," but there are other excuses, as most men know, and when the white world objects to black women because it does not consider them beautiful, the black world of right asks two questions: "What is beauty?" and, "Suppose you think them ugly, what then? If ugliness and unconventionality and eccentricity of face and deed do not hinder men from doing the world's work and reaping the world's reward, why should it hinder women?"

Other things being equal, all of us, black and white, would prefer to be beautiful in face and form and suitably clothed; but most of us are not so, and one of the mightiest revolts of the century is against the devilish decree that no woman is a woman who is not by present standards a beautiful woman. This decree the black women of America have in large measure escaped from the first. Not being expected to be merely ornamental, they have girded themselves for work, instead of adorning their bodies only for play. Their sturdier minds have concluded that if a woman be clean, healthy, and educated, she is as pleasing as God wills and far more useful than most of her sisters. If in addition to this she is pink and white and straight-haired, and some of her fellow-men prefer this, well and good; but if she is black or brown and crowned in curled mists (and this to us is the most beautiful thing on earth), this is surely the flimsiest excuse for spiritual incarceration or banishment.

The very attempt to do this in the case of Negro Americans has strangely over-reached itself. By so much as the defective eyesight of the white world rejects black women as beauties, by so much the more it needs them as human beings,—an enviable alternative, as many a white woman knows. Consequently, for black women alone, as a group, "handsome is that handsome does" and they are asked to be no more beautiful than God made them, but they are asked to be efficient, to be strong, fertile, muscled, and able to work. If they marry, they must as independent workers be able to help support their children, for their men are paid on a scale which makes sole support of the family often impossible.

On the whole, colored working women are paid as well as white working women for similar work, save in some higher grades, while colored men get from one-fourth to three-fourths less than white men. The result is curious and three-fold: the economic independence of black women is increased, the breaking up of Negro families must be more frequent, and the number of illegitimate children is decreased more slowly among them than other evidences of culture are increased, just as was once true in Scotland and Bavaria.

What does this mean? It forecasts a mighty dilemma which the whole world of civilization, despite its will, must one time frankly face: the unhusbanded mother or the childless wife. God send us a world with woman's freedom and married motherhood inextricably wed, but until He sends it, I see more of future promise in the betrayed girl-mothers of the black belt than in the childless wives of the white North, and I have more respect for the colored servant who yields to her frank longing for motherhood than for her white sister who offers up children for clothes. Out of a sex freedom that today makes us shudder will come in time a day when we will no longer pay men for work they

do not do, for the sake of their harem; we will pay women
what they earn and insist on their working and earning it;
we will allow those persons to vote who know enough to
vote, whether they be black or female, white or male; and
we will ward race suicide, not by further burdening the
over-burdened, but by honoring motherhood, even when
the sneaking father shirks his duty.

"Wait till the lady passes," said a Nashville white boy.

"She's no lady; she's a nigger," answered another.

So some few women are born free, and some amid insult
and scarlet letters achieve freedom; but our women in black
had freedom thrust contemptuously upon them. With that
freedom they are buying an untrammeled independence and
dear as is the price they pay for it, it will in the end be worth
every taunt and groan. Today the dreams of the mothers are
coming true. We have still our poverty and degradation, our
lewdness and our cruel toil; but we have, too, a vast group of
women of Negro blood who for strength of character,
cleanness of soul, and unselfish devotion of purpose, is today
easily the peer of any group of women in the civilized
world. And more than that, in the great rank and file of our
five million women we have the up-working of new revolutionary ideals, which must in time have vast influence on
the thought and action of this land.

For this, their promise, and for their hard past, I honor
the women of my race. Their beauty,—their dark and mysterious beauty of midnight eyes, crumpled hair, and soft,
full-featured faces—is perhaps more to me than to you,
because I was born to its warm and subtle spell; but their
worth is yours as well as mine. No other women on earth
could have emerged from the hell of force and temptation
which once engulfed and still surrounds black women in
America with half the modesty and womanliness that they

retain. I have always felt like bowing myself before them in all abasement, searching to bring some tribute to these long-suffering victims, these burdened sisters of mine, whom the world, the wise, white world, loves to affront and ridicule and wantonly to insult. I have known the women of many lands and nations,—I have known and seen and lived beside them, but none have I known more sweetly feminine, more unswervingly loyal, more desperately earnest, and more instinctively pure in body and in soul than the daughters of my black mothers. This, then,—a little thing—to their memory and inspiration.

Children of the Moon

I am dead;
Yet somehow, somewhere,
In Time's weird contradiction, I
May tell of that dread deed, wherewith
I brought to Children of the Moon
Freedom and vast salvation.

I was a woman born,
And trod the streaming street,
That ebbs and flows from Harlem's hills,
Through caves and canons limned in light,
Down to the twisting sea.

That night of nights,
I stood alone and at the End,
Until the sudden highway to the moon,
Golden in splendor,
Became too real to doubt.

Dimly I set foot upon the air,
I fled, I flew, through thrills of light,
With all about, above, below, the whirring
Of almighty wings.

I found a twilight land,
Where, hardly hid, the sun
Sent softly-saddened rays of
Red and brown to burn the iron soil
And bathe the snow-white peaks
In mighty splendor.

Black were the men,
Hard-haired and silent-slow,
Moving as shadows,
Bending with face of fear to earthward;
And women there were none.

"Woman, woman, woman!"
I cried in mounting terror.
"Woman and Child!"
And the cry sang back
Through heaven, with the
Whirring of almighty wings.

Wings, wings, endless wings,—
Heaven and earth are wings;
Wings that flutter, furl, and fold,
Always folding and unfolding,
Ever folding yet again;
Wings, veiling some vast
And veiled face,
In blazing blackness,
Behind the folding and unfolding,
The rolling and unrolling of
Almighty wings!

I saw the black men huddle,
Fumed in fear, falling face downward;

Vainly I clutched and clawed,
Dumbly they cringed and cowered,
Moaning in mournful monotone:

O Freedom, O Freedom,
O Freedom over me;
Before I'll be a slave,
I'll be buried in my grave,
And go home to my God,
And be free.

It was as angel-music
From the dead,
And ever, as they sang,
Some wingéd thing of wings, filling all heaven,
Folding and unfolding, and folding yet again,
Tore out their blood and entrails,
'Til I screamed in utter terror;
And a silence came,—
A silence and the wailing of a babe.

Then, at last, I saw and shamed;
I knew how these dumb, dark, and dusky things
Had given blood and life,
To fend the caves of underground,
The great black caves of utter night,
Where earth lay full of mothers
And their babes.

Little children sobbing in darkness,
Little children crying in silent pain,
Little mothers rocking and groping and struggling,
Digging and delving and groveling,

Amid the dying-dead and dead-in-life
And drip and dripping of warm, wet blood,
Far, far beneath the wings,—
The folding and unfolding of almighty wings.

I bent with tears and pitying hands,
Above these dusky star-eyed children,—
Crinkly-haired, with sweet-sad baby voices,
Pleading low for light and love and living—
And I crooned:

"Little children weeping there,
God shall find your faces fair;
Guerdon for your deep distress,
He shall send His tenderness;

For the tripping of your feet
Make a mystic music sweet
In the darkness of your hair;
Light and laughter in the air—
Little children weeping there,
God shall find your faces fair!"

I strode above the stricken, bleeding men,
The rampart 'ranged against the skies,
And shouted:
"Up, I say, build and slay;
Fight face foremost, force a way,
Unloose, unfetter, and unbind;
Be men and free!"

Dumbly they shrank,
Muttering they pointed toward that peak,

Than vastness vaster,
Whereon a darkness brooded,
"Who shall look and live," they sighed;
And I sensed
The folding and unfolding of almighty wings.

Yet did we build of iron, bricks, and blood;
We built a day, a year, a thousand years,
Blood was the mortar,—blood and tears,
And, ah, the Thing, the Thing of wings,
The wingéd, folding Wing of Things
Did furnish much mad mortar
For that tower.

Slow and ever slower rose the towering task,
And with it rose the sun,
Until at last on one wild day,
Wind-whirled, cloud-swept and terrible
I stood beneath the burning shadow
Of the peak,
Beneath the whirring of almighty wings,
While downward from my feet
Streamed the long line of dusky faces
And the wail of little children sobbing under earth.

Alone, aloft,
I saw through firmaments on high
The drama of Almighty God,
With all its flaming suns and stars.
"Freedom!" I cried.
"Freedom!" cried heaven, earth, and stars;
And a Voice near-far,
Amid the folding and unfolding of almighty wings,

Answered, "I am Freedom—
Who sees my face is free—
He and his."

I dared not look;
Downward I glanced on deep-bowed heads and closéd eyes,
Outward I gazed on flecked and flaming blue—
But ever onward, upward flew
The sobbing of small voices,—
Down, down, far down into the night.

Slowly I lifted livid limbs aloft;
Upward I strove: the face! the face!
Onward I reeled: the face! the face!
To beauty wonderful as sudden death,
Or horror horrible as endless life—
Up! Up! the blood-built way;
(Shadow grow vaster!
Terror come faster!)
Up! Up! to the blazing blackness
Of one veiléd face.

And endless folding and unfolding,
Rolling and unrolling of almighty wings.
The last step stood!
The last dim cry of pain
Fluttered across the stars,
And then—
Wings, wings, triumphant wings,
Lifting and lowering, waxing and waning,
Swinging and swaying, twirling and whirling,
Whispering and screaming, streaming and gleaming,
Spreading and sweeping and shading and flaming—
Wings, wings, eternal wings,

'Til the hot, red blood,
Flood fleeing flood,
Thundered through heaven and mine ears,
While all across a purple sky,
The last vast pinion
Trembled to unfold.

I rose upon the Mountain of the Moon,—
I felt the blazing glory of the Sun;
I heard the Song of Children crying, "Free!"
I saw the face of Freedom—
And I died.

VIII | THE IMMORTAL CHILD

I F a man die shall he live again? We do not know. But this we do know, that our children's children live forever and grow and develop toward perfection as they are trained. All human problems, then, center in the Immortal Child and his education is the problem of problems. And first for illustration of what I would say may I not take for example, out of many millions, the life of one dark child.

It is now nineteen years since I first saw Coleridge-Taylor. We were in London in some somber hall where there were many meeting, men and women called chiefly to the beautiful World's Fair at Paris; and then a few slipping over to London to meet Pan-Africa. We were there from Cape Colony and Liberia, from Haiti and the States, and from the Islands of the Sea. I remember the stiff, young officer who came with credentials from Menelik of Abyssinia; I remember the bitter, black American who whispered how an army of the Soudan might some day cross the Alps; I remember Englishmen, like the Colensos, who sat and counseled with us; but above all, I remember Coleridge-Taylor.

He was a little man and nervous, with dark-golden face and hair that bushed and strayed. His fingers were always nervously seeking hidden keys and he was quick with enthusiasm,—instinct with life. His bride of a year or more,—dark, too, in her whiter way,—was of the calm and quiet type. Her soft contralto voice thrilled us often as she sang, while her silences were full of understanding.

Several times we met in public gatherings and then they bade me to their home,—a nest of a cottage, with gate and garden, hidden in London's endless rings of suburbs. I dimly recall through these years a room in cozy disorder, strewn with music—music on the floor and music on the chairs, music in the air as the master rushed to the piano now and again to make some memory melodious—some allusion real.

And then at last, for it was the last, I saw Coleridge-Taylor in a mighty throng of people crowding the Crystal Palace. We came in facing the stage and scarcely dared look around. On the stage were a full orchestra, a chorus of eight hundred voices, and some of the world's famous soloists. He left his wife sitting beside me, and she was very silent as he went forward to lift the conductor's baton. It was one of the earliest renditions of "Hiawatha's Wedding Feast." We sat at rapt attention and when the last, weird music died, the great chorus and orchestra rose as a man to acclaim the master; he turned toward the audience and then we turning for the first time saw that sea of faces behind,—the misty thousands whose voices rose to one strong shout of joy! It was a moment such as one does not often live. It seemed, and was, prophetic.

This young man who stepped forth as one of the most notable of modern English composers had a simple and uneventful career. His father was a black surgeon of Sierra Leone who came to London for study. While there he met an English girl and this son was born, in London, in 1875.

Then came a series of chances. His father failed to succeed and disappeared back to Africa leaving the support of the child to the poor working mother. The child showed evidences of musical talent and a friendly workingman gave him a little violin. A musician glancing from his window saw a little dark boy playing marbles on the street with a tiny violin in one hand; he gave him lessons. He happened to gain entrance into a charity school with a master of understanding mind who recognized genius when he saw it; and finally his beautiful child's treble brought him to the notice of the choirmaster of St. George's, Croyden.

So by happy accident his way was clear. Within his soul was no hesitation. He was one of those fortunate beings who are not called to *Wander-Jahre*, but are born with sails set and seas charted. Already the baby of four little years was a musician, and as choir-boy and violinist he walked unhesitatingly and surely to his life work. He was graduated with honors from the Royal Academy of Music in 1894, and married soon after the daughter of one of his professors. Then his life began, and whatever it lacked of physical adventure in the conventional round of a modern world-city, it more than gained in the almost tempestuous outpouring of his spiritual nature. Life to him was neither meat nor drink,—it was creative flame; ideas, plans, melodies glowed within him. To create, to do, to accomplish; to know the white glory of mighty midnights and the pale Amen of dawns was his day of days. Songs, pianoforte and violin pieces, trios and quintets for strings, incidental music, symphony, orchestral, and choral works rushed from his fingers. Nor were they laboriously contrived or light, thin things made to meet sudden popularity. Rather they were the flaming bits that must be said and sung,—that could not wait the slower birth of years, so hurried to the world as though their young creator knew that God gave him but a day. His whole active life was scarcely more than a decade and a half, and yet in that time, without wealth, friends, or influence, in the face of perhaps the most critical and skeptical and least imaginative civilization of the modern world, he wrote his name so high as a creative artist that it cannot soon be forgotten.

And this was but one side of the man. On the other was the sweet-tempered, sympathetic comrade, always willing to help, never knowing how to refuse, generous with every nerve and fiber of his being. Think of a young musician, father of a family, who at the time of his death held positions as Associate of the Royal College of Music, Professor in Trinity College and Crystal Palace, Conductor of the Handel Choral Society and the Rochester Choral Society, Principal of the Guildhall School of Music, where he had charge of the choral choir, the orchestra, and the opera. He was repeatedly the leader of music festivals all over Great Britain and a judge of contests. And with all this his house was open in cheering hospitality to friends and his hand ever ready with sympathy and help.

When such a man dies, it must bring pause to a reasoning world. We may call his death-sickness pneumonia, but we all know that it was sheer overwork,—the using of a delicately-tuned instrument too commonly and continuously and carelessly to let it last its normal life. We may well talk of the waste of wood and water, of food and fire, but the real and unforgivable waste of modern civilization is the waste of ability and genius,—the killing of useful, indispensable men who have no right to die; who deserve, not for themselves, but for the world, leisure, freedom from distraction, expert medical advice, and intelligent sympathy.

Coleridge-Taylor's life work was not finished,—it was

but well begun. He lived only his first period of creative genius, when melody and harmony flashed and fluttered in subtle, compelling, and more than promising profusion. He did not live to do the organized, constructive work in the full, calm power of noonday,—the reflective finishing of evening. In the annals of the future his name must always stand high, but with the priceless gift of years, who can say where it might not have stood.

Why should he have worked so breathlessly, almost furiously? It was, we may be sure, because with unflinching determination and with no thought of surrender he faced the great alternative,—the choice which the cynical, thoughtless, busy, modern world spreads grimly before its greater souls—food or beauty, bread and butter, or ideals. And continually we see worthier men turning to the pettier, cheaper thing—the popular portrait, the sensational novel, the jingling song. The choice is not always between the least and the greatest, the high and the empty, but only too often it is between starvation and something. When, therefore, we see a man, working desperately to earn a living and still stooping to no paltry dickering and to no unworthy work, handing away a "Hiawatha" for less than a song, pausing for glimpses of the stars when a world full of charcoal glowed far more warmly and comfortably, we know that such a man is a hero in a sense never approached by the swashbuckling soldier or the lying patriot.

Deep as was the primal tragedy in the life of Coleridge-Taylor, there lay another still deeper. He smiled at it lightly, as we all do,—we who live within the veil,—to hide the deeper hurt. He had, with us, that divine and African gift of laughter, that echo of a thousand centuries of suns. I mind me how once he told of the bishop, the well-groomed English bishop, who eyed the artist gravely, with his eye-glass—hair and color and figure,—and said quite audibly to his friends, "Quite interesting—looks intelligent,—yes—yes!"

Fortunate was Coleridge-Taylor to be born in Europe and to speak a universal tongue. In America he could hardly have had his career. His genius was, to be sure, recognized (with some palpitation and consternation) when it came full-grown across the seas with an English imprint; but born here, it might never have been permitted to grow. We know in America how to discourage, choke, and murder ability when it so far forgets itself as to choose a dark skin. England, thank God, is slightly more civilized than her colonies; but even there the path of this young man was no way of roses and just a shade thornier than that of whiter men. He did not complain at it,—he did not

"Wince and cry aloud."

Rather the hint here and there of color discrimination in England aroused in him deeper and more poignant sympathy with his people throughout the world. He was one with that great company of mixed-blooded men: Pushkin and Dumas, Hamilton and Douglass, Browning and many others; but he more than most of these men knew the call of the blood when it came and listened and answered. He came to America with strange enthusiasm. He took with quite simple and unconscious grace the conventional congratulations of the musical world. He was used to that. But to his own people—to the sad sweetness of their voices, their inborn sense of music, their broken, half-articulate voices,—he leapt with new enthusiasm. From the fainter shadowings of his own life, he sensed instinctively the vaster tragedy of theirs. His soul yearned to give voice and being to this human thing. He early turned to the sorrow songs. He sat at the faltering feet of Paul Laurence Dunbar and he asked (as we sadly shook our heads) for some masterpiece of this world-tragedy that his soul could set to music. And then, so characteristically, he rushed back to England, composed a half-dozen exquisite harmonies haunted by slave-songs, led the Welsh in their singing, listened to the Scotch, ordered great music festivals in all England, wrote for Beer-bohm Tree, took on another music professorship, promised a trip to Germany, and at last, staggering home one night, on his way to his wife and little boy and girl, fell in his tracks and in four days was dead, at the age of thirty-seven. They say that in his death-throe he arose and facing some great, ghostly choir raised his last baton, while all around the massive silence rang with the last mist-music of his dying ears.

He was buried from St. Michael's on September 5, 1912, with the acclaim of kings and music masters and little children and to the majestic melody of his own music. The tributes that followed him to his grave were unusually hearty and sincere. The head of the Royal College calls the first production of "Hiawatha" one of the most remarkable events in modern English musical history and the trilogy one of the most universally-beloved works of modern English music. One critic calls Taylor's a name "which with that of Elgar represented the nation's most individual output" and calls his "Atonement" "perhaps the finest passion music of modern times." Another critic speaks of his originality: "Though surrounded by the influences that are at work in Europe today, he retained his individuality to the end, developing his style, however, and evincing new ideas in each succeeding work. His untimely death at the age of thirty-seven, a short life—like those of Schubert, Mendelssohn, Chopin, and Hugo Wolf—has robbed the world of one of its noblest singers, one of those few men of modern times who found expression in the language of musical song, a lyricist of power and worth."

But the tributes did not rest with the artist; with peculiar unanimity they sought his "sterling character," "the good husband and father," the "staunch and loyal friend." And perhaps I cannot better end these hesitating words than with that tribute from one who called this master, friend, and whose lament cried in the night with more of depth and passion than Alfred Noyes is wont in his self-repression to voice:

> "Through him, his race, a moment, lifted up
> Forests of hands to beauty, as in prayer,
> Touched through his lips the sacramental cup
> And then sank back, benumbed in our bleak air."

Yet, consider: to many millions of people this man was all wrong. *First*, he ought never to have been born, for he was the mulatto son of a white woman. *Secondly*, he should never have been educated as a musician,—he should have been trained for his "place" in the world and to make him satisfied therewith. *Thirdly*, he should not have married the woman he loved and who loved him, for she was white and the niece of an Oxford professor. Fourthly, the children of such a union—but why proceed? You know it all by heart.

If he had been black, like Paul Laurence Dunbar, would the argument have been different? No. He should never have been born, for he is a "problem." He should never be educated, for he cannot be educated. He should never marry, for that means children and there is no place for black children in this world.

In the treatment of the child the world foreshadows its own future and faith. All words and all thinking lead to the child,—to that vast immortality and wide sweep of infinite possibility which the child represents. Such thought as this it was that made the Master say of old as He saw baby faces:

"And whosoever shall offend one of these little ones, it is better for him that a millstone were hanged about his neck and he were cast into the sea."

And yet the mothers and fathers and the men and women of my race must often pause and ask: Is it worth while? Ought children be born to us? Have we any right to make human souls face what we face today? The answer is clear: If the great battle of human right against poverty, against disease, against color prejudice is to be won, it must be won, not in our day, but in the day of our children's children. Ours is the blood and dust of battle; theirs the rewards of victory. If, then, they are not there because we have not brought them into the world, we have been the guiltiest factor in conquering ourselves. It is our duty, then, to accomplish the immortality of black blood, in order that the day may come in this dark world when poverty shall be abolished, privilege be based on individual desert, and the color of a man's skin be no bar to the outlook of his soul.

If it is our duty as honest colored men and women, battling for a great principle, to bring not aimless rafts of children to the world, but as many as, with reasonable sacrifice, we can train to largest manhood, what in its inner essence shall that training be, particularly in its beginning?

The first temptation is to shield the child,—to hedge it about that it may not know and will not dream of the color line. Then when we can no longer wholly shield, to indulge and pamper and coddle, as though in this dumb way to compensate. From this attitude comes the multitude of our spoiled, wayward, disappointed children. And must we not blame ourselves? For while the motive was pure and the outer menace undoubted, is shielding and indulgence the way to meet it?

Some Negro parents, realizing this, leave their children to sink or swim in this sea of race prejudice. They neither shield nor explain, but thrust them forth grimly into school or street and let them learn as they may from brutal fact. Out of this may come strength, poise, self-dependence, and out of it, too, may come bewilderment, cringing deception, and self-distrust. It is, all said, a brutal, unfair method, and in its way it is as bad as shielding and indulgence. Why not, rather, face the facts and tell the truth? Your child is wiser than you think.

The truth lies ever between extremes. It is wrong to introduce the child to race consciousness prematurely; it is dangerous to let that consciousness grow spontaneously without intelligent guidance. With every step of dawning intelligence, explanation—frank, free, guiding explanation—must come. The day will dawn when mother must explain gently but clearly why the little girls next door do not want to play with "niggers"; what the real cause is of the teachers' unsympathetic attitude; and how people may ride in the backs of street cars and the smoker end of trains and still be people, honest high-minded souls.

Remember, too, that in such frank explanation you are speaking in nine cases out of ten to a good deal clearer understanding than you think and that the child-mind has what your tired soul may have lost faith in,—the Power, and the Glory.

Out of little, unspoiled souls rise up wonderful resources and healing balm. Once the colored child understands the white world's attitude and the shameful wrong of it, you have furnished it with a great life motive,—a power and impulse toward good which is the mightiest thing man has. How many white folk would give their own souls if they might graft into their children's souls a great, moving, guiding ideal!

With this Power there comes, in the transfiguring soul of childhood, the Glory: the vision of accomplishment, the lofty ideal. Once let the strength of the motive work, and it becomes the life task of the parent to guide and to shape the ideal; to raise it from resentment and revenge to dignity and self-respect, to breadth and accomplishment, to human service; to beat back every thought of cringing and surrender.

Here, at last, we can speak with no hesitation, with no lack of faith. For we know that as the world grows better there will be realized in our children's lives that for which we fight unfalteringly, but vainly now.

So much for the problem of the home and our own dark children. Now let us look beyond the pale upon the children of the wide world. What is the real lesson of the life of Coleridge-Taylor? It is this: humanly speaking it was sheer accident that this boy developed his genius. We have a right to assume that hundreds and thousands of boys and girls today are missing the chance of developing unusual talents because the chances have been against them; and that indeed the majority of the children of the world are not being systematically fitted for their life work and for life itself. Why?

Many seek the reason in the content of the school program. They feverishly argue the relative values of Greek, mathematics, and manual training, but fail with singular unanimity in pointing out the fundamental cause of our failure in human education: That failure is due to the fact that we aim not at the full development of the child, but that the world regards and always has regarded education first as a means of buttressing the established order of things rather than improving it. And this is the real reason why strife, war, and revolution have marked the onward march of humanity instead of reason and sound reform. Instead of seeking to push the coming generation ahead of our pitiful accomplishment, we insist that it march behind. We say, morally, that high character is conformity to present public opinion; we say industrially that the present order is best and that children must be trained to perpetuate it.

But, it is objected, what else can we do? Can we teach Revolution to the inexperienced in hope that they may discern progress? No, but we may teach frankly that this world is not perfection, but development: that the object of education is manhood and womanhood, clear reason, individual talent and genius and the spirit of service and sacrifice, and not simply a frantic effort to avoid change in present institutions; that industry is for man and not man for industry and that while we must have workers to work, the prime object of our training is not the work but the worker—not the maintenance of present industrial caste but the development of human intelligence by which drudgery may be lessened and beauty widened.

Back of our present educational system is the philosophy that sneers at the foolish Fathers who believed it self-evident, "that all men were created free and equal." Surely the overwhelming evidence is today that men are slaves and unequal. But is it not education that is the creator of this freedom and equality? Most men today cannot conceive of a freedom that does not involve somebody's slavery. They do not want equality because the thrill of their happiness comes from having things that others have not. But may not human education fix the fine ideal of an equal maximum of freedom for every human soul combined with that minimum of slavery for each soul which the inexorable physical facts of the world impose—rather than complete freedom for some and complete slavery for others; and, again, is not the equality toward which the world moves an equality of honor in the assigned human task itself rather than equal facility in doing different tasks? Human equality is not lack of difference, nor do the infinite human differences argue relative superiority and inferiority. And, again, how new an aspect human differences may assume when all men are educated. Today we think of apes, semi-apes, and human beings; tomorrow we may think of Keir Hardies, Roosevelts, and Beethovens—not equals but men. Today we are forcing men into educational slavery in order that others may enjoy life, and excuse ourselves by saying that the world's work must be done. We are degrading some sorts of work by honoring others, and then expressing surprise that most people object to having their children trained solely to take up their father's tasks.

Given as the ideal the utmost possible freedom for every human soul, with slavery for none, and equal honor for all necessary human tasks, then our problem of education is greatly simplified: we aim to develop human souls; to make all intelligent; to discover special talents and genius. With this course of training beginning in early childhood and never ceasing must go the technical training for the present world's work according to carefully studied individual gifts and wishes.

On the other hand, if we arrange our system of education to develop workmen who will not strike and Negroes satisfied with their present place in the world, we have set ourselves a baffling task. We find ourselves compelled to keep the masses ignorant and to curb our own thought and expression so as not to inflame the ignorant. We force moderate reformers and men with new and valuable ideas to become red radicals and revolutionists, since that happens to be the only way to make the world listen to reason. Consider our race problem in the South: the South has invested in Negro ignorance; some Northerners proposed limited education, not, they explained, to better the Negro, but merely to make the investment more profitable to the present beneficiaries. They thus gained wide Southern support for schools like Hampton and Tuskegee. But could this program be expected long to satisfy colored folk? And was this shifty dodging of the real issue the wisest statesmanship? No! The real question in the South is the question of the permanency of present color caste. The problem, then, of the formal training of our colored children has been strangely complicated by the strong feeling of certain persons as to their future in America and the world. And the reaction toward this caste education has strengthened the idea of caste education throughout the world.

Let us then return to fundamental ideals. Children must be trained in a knowledge of what the world is and what it knows and how it does its daily work. These things cannot be separated: we cannot teach pure knowledge apart from actual facts, or separate truth from the human mind. Above all we must not forget that the object of all education is the child itself and not what it does or makes.

It is here that a great movement in America has grievously sinned against the light. There has arisen among us a movement to make the Public School primarily the handmaiden of production. America is conceived of as existing for the sake of its mines, fields and factories, and not those factories, fields and mines as existing for America. Consequently, the public schools are for training the mass of men as servants and laborers and mechanics to increase the land's industrial efficiency.

Those who oppose this program, especially if they are black, are accused of despising common toil and humble service. In fact, we Negroes are but facing in our own children a world problem: how can we, while maintaining a proper output of goods and furnishing needed services, increase the knowledge of experience of common men and conserve genius for the common weal? Without wider, deeper intelligence among the masses Democracy cannot accomplish its greater ends. Without a more careful conservation of human ability and talent the world cannot secure the services which its greater needs call for. Yet today who goes to college, the Talented or the Rich? Who goes to high school, the Bright or the Well-to-Do? Who does the physical work of the world, those whose muscles need the exercise or those whose souls and minds are stupefied with manual toil? How is the drudgery of the world distributed, by thoughtful justice or the lash of Slavery?

We cannot base the education of future citizens on the present inexcusable inequality of wealth nor on physical differences of race. We must seek not to make men carpenters but to make carpenters men.

Colored Americans must then with deep determination educate their children in the broadest, highest way. They must fill the colleges with the talented and fill the fields and shops with the intelligent. Wisdom is the principal thing. Therefore, get wisdom.

But why am I talking simply of "colored" children? Is not the problem of their education simply an intensification of the problem of educating all children? Look at our plight in the United States, nearly 150 years after the establishment of a government based on human intelligence.

If we take the figures of the Thirteenth Census, we find that there were five and one-half million illiterate Ameri-

cans of whom 3,184,633 were white. Remembering that
illiteracy is a crude and extreme test of ignorance, we may
assume that there are in the United States ten million people
over ten years of age who are too ignorant either to perform
their civic duties or to teach industrial efficiency. Moreover,
it does not seem that this illiteracy is disappearing rapidly.

For instance, nine percent of American children
between ten and nineteen years of age cannot read and
write. Moreover, there are millions of children who,
judging by the figures for the school year 1909–10, are not
going to learn to read and write, for of the Americans six
to fourteen years of age there were 3,125,392 who were not
in school a single day during that year. If we take the eleven
million youths fifteen to twenty years of age for whom
vocational training is particularly adapted, we find that
nearly five percent of these, or 448,414, are absolutely illiterate; it is not too much to assume that a million of them
have not acquired enough of the ordinary tools of intelligence to make the most of efficient vocational training.

Confining ourselves to the white people, over fifteen
percent of the white children six to fourteen years of age,
or 2,253,198, did not attend school during the school year
1909–10. Of the native white children of native parents ten
to fourteen years of age nearly a tenth were not in school
during that year; 121,878 native white children of native
parents, fifteen to nineteen years of age, were illiterate.

If we confine our attention to the colored children, the
case is, of course, much worse.

We cannot hope to make intelligent workmen and
intelligent citizens of a group of people, over forty percent
of whose children six to fourteen years of age were not in
school a single day during 1909–10; for the other sixty percent the school term in the majority of cases was probably

less than five months. Of the Negro children ten to fourteen years of age 18.9 percent were illiterate; of those fifteen to nineteen years of age 20.3 percent were illiterate; of those ten to fourteen years of age 31.4 percent did not go to school a single day in 1909–10.

What is the trouble? It is simple. We are spending one dollar for education where we should spend ten dollars. If tomorrow we multiplied our effort to educate the next generation ten-fold, we should but begin our bounden duty. The heaven that lies about our infancy is but the ideals come true which every generation of children is capable of bringing; but we, selfish in our own ignorance and incapacity, are making of education a series of miserable compromises: How ignorant can we let a child grow to be in order to make him the best cotton mill operative? What is the least sum that will keep the average youth out of jail? How many months saved on a high school course will make the largest export of wheat?

If we realized that children are the future, that immortality is the present child, that no education which educates can possibly be too costly, then we know that the menace of Kaiserism which called for the expenditure of more than 332 thousand millions of dollars was not a whit more pressing than the menace of ignorance, and that no nation tomorrow will call itself civilized which does not give every single human being college and vocational training free and under the best teaching force procurable for love or money.

This world has never taken the education of children seriously. Misled by selfish dreamings of personal life forever, we have neglected the true and practical immortality through the endless life of children's children. Seeking counsels of our own souls' perfection, we have despised and rejected the possible increasing perfection of unending generations. Or if we are thrown back in pessimistic despair from making living folk decent, we leap to idle speculations of a thousand years hereafter instead of working steadily and persistently for the next generation.

All our problems center in the child. All our hopes, our dreams are for our children. Has our own life failed? Let its lesson save the children's lives from similar failure. Is democracy a failure? Train up citizens that will make it succeed. Is wealth too crude, too foolish in form, and too easily stolen? Train up workers with honor and consciences and brains. Have we degraded service with menials? Abolish the mean spirit and implant sacrifice. Do we despise women? Train them as workers and thinkers and not as playthings, lest future generations ape our worst mistake. Do we despise darker races? Teach the children its fatal cost in spiritual degradation and murder, teach them that to hate "niggers" or "chinks" is to crucify souls like their own. Is there anything we would accomplish with human beings? Do it with the immortal child, with a stretch of endless time for doing it and with infinite possibilities to work on.

Is this our attitude toward education? It is not—neither in England nor America—in France nor Germany—with black nor white nor yellow folk. Education to the modern world is a burden which we are driven to carry. We shirk and complain. We do just as little as possible and only threat or catastrophe induces us to do more than a minimum. If the ignorant mass, panting to know, revolts, we dole them gingerly enough knowledge to pacify them temporarily. If, as in the Great War, we discover soldiers too ignorant to use our machines of murder and destruction, we train them— to use machines of murder and destruction. If mounting wealth calls for intelligent workmen, we rush tumultuously to train workers—in order to increase our wealth. But of great, broad plans to train all men for all things—to make a universe intelligent, busy, good, creative and beautiful—where in this wide world is such an educational program? To announce it is to invite gasps or Brobdingnagian laughter. It cannot be done. It will cost too much.

What has been done with man can be done with men, if the world tries long enough and hard enough. And as to the cost—all the wealth of the world, save that necessary for sheer decent existence and for the maintenance of past civilization, is, and of right ought to be, the property of the children for their education.

I mean it. In one year, 1917, we spent $96,700,000,000 for war. We blew it away to murder, maim, and destroy! Why? Because the blind, brutal crime of powerful and selfish interests made this path through hell the only visible way to heaven. We did it. We had to do it, and we are glad the putrid horror is over. But, now, are we prepared to spend less to make a world in which the resurgence of such devilish power will be impossible?

Do we really want war to cease?

Then educate the children of this generation at a cost no whit less and if necessary a hundred times as great as the cost of the Great War.

Last year, 1917, education cost us $915,000,000.

Next year it ought to cost us at least two thousand million dollars. We should spend enough money to hire the best teaching force possible—the best organizing and directing ability in the land, even if we have to strip the railroads and meat trust. We should dot city and country with the most efficient, sanitary, and beautiful school-houses the world knows and we should give every American child common school, high school, and college training and then vocational guidance in earning a living.

Is this a dream?

Can we afford less?

Consider our so-called educational "problems": "How may we keep pupils in the high school?" Feed and clothe them. "Shall we teach Latin, Greek, and mathematics to the 'masses'?" If they are worth teaching to anybody, the masses need them most. "Who shall go to college?" Everybody. "When shall culture training give place to technical education for work?" Never.

These questions are not "problems." They are simply "excuses" for spending less time and money on the next generation. Given ten millions of dollars a year, what can we best do with the education of a million children? The real answer is—kill nine hundred and ninety thousand of them quickly and not gradually, and make thoroughly-trained men and women of the other ten thousand. But who set the limit of ten million dollars? Who says it shall not be ten thousand millions, as it ought to be? You and I say it, and in saying it we sin against the Holy Ghost.

We sin because in our befuddled brains we have linked money and education inextricably. We assume that only the wealthy have a real right to education when, in fact, being born is being given a right to college training. Our wealth today is, we all know, distributed mainly by chance inheritance and personal favor and yet we attempt to base the right to education on this foundation. The result is grotesque! We bury genius; we send it to jail; we ridicule and mock it, while we send mediocrity and idiocy to college, gilded and crowned. For three hundred years we have denied black Americans an education and now we exploit them before a gaping world: See how ignorant and degraded they are! All they are fit for is education for cotton-picking and dish-washing. When Dunbar and Taylor happen along, we are torn between something like shamefaced anger or impatient amazement.

A world guilty of this last and mightiest war has no right to enjoy or create until it has made the future safe from another Arkansas or Rheims. To this there is but one patent way, proved and inescapable, Education, and that not for me or for you but for the Immortal Child. And that child is of all races and all colors. All children are the children of all and not of individuals and families and races. The whole generation must be trained and guided and out of it as out of a huge reservoir must be lifted all genius, talent, and intelligence to serve all the world.

*Almighty Death**

Softly, quite softly—
For I hear, above the murmur of the sea,
Faint and far-fallen footsteps, as of One
Who comes from out beyond the endless ends of Time,
With voice that downward looms thro' singing stars;
Its subtle sound I see thro' these long-darkened eyes,
I hear the Light He bringeth on His hands—
Almighty Death!
Softly, oh, softly, lest He pass me by,
And that unquivering Light toward which my longing soul
And tortured body through these years have writhed,
Fade to the dun darkness of my days.

Softly, full softly, let me rise and greet
The strong, low luting of that long-awaited call;
Swiftly be all my good and going gone,
And this vast veiled and vanquished vigor of my soul
Seek somehow otherwhere its rest and goal,
Where endless spaces stretch,
Where endless time doth moan,
Where endless light doth pour
Thro' the black kingdoms of eternal death.

---

*For Joseph Pulitzer, October 29, 1911.

Then haply I may see what things I have not seen,
Then I may know what things I have not known;
Then may I do my dreams.
Farewell! No sound of idle mourning let there be
To shudder this full silence—save the voice
Of children—little children, white and black,
Whispering the deeds I tried to do for them;
While I at last unguided and alone
Pass softly, full softly.

IX | OF BEAUTY AND DEATH

FOR long years we of the world gone wild have looked into the face of death and smiled. Through all our bitter tears we knew how beautiful it was to die for that which our souls called sufficient. Like all true beauty this thing of dying was so simple, so matter-of-fact. The boy clothed in his splendid youth stood before us and laughed in his own jolly way,—went and was gone. Suddenly the world was full of the fragrance of sacrifice. We left our digging and burden-bearing; we turned from our scraping and twisting of things and words; we paused from our hurrying hither and thither and walking up and down, and asked in half-whisper: this Death—is this Life? And is its beauty real or false? And of this heart-questioning I am writing.

My friend, who is pale and positive, said to me yesterday, as the tired sun was nodding:

"You are too sensitive."

I admit, I am—sensitive. I am artificial. I cringe or am bumptious or immobile. I am intellectually dishonest, art-blind, and I lack humor.

"Why don't you stop all this?" she retorts triumphantly. You will not let us.

"There you go, again. You know that I—"

Wait! I answer. Wait!

I arise at seven. The milkman has neglected me. He pays little attention to colored districts. My white neighbor glares elaborately. I walk softly, lest I disturb him. The children jeer as I pass to work. The women in the street car withdraw their skirts or prefer to stand. The policeman is truculent. The elevator man hates to serve Negroes. My job is insecure because the white union wants it and does not want me. I try to lunch, but no place near will serve me. I go forty blocks to Marshall's, but the Committee of Fourteen closes Marshall's; they say white women frequent it.

"Do all eating places discriminate?"

No, but how shall I know which do not—except—

I hurry home through crowds. They mutter or get angry. I go to a mass-meeting. They stare. I go to a church. "We don't admit niggers!"

Or perhaps I leave the beaten track. I seek new work. "Our employees would not work with you; our customers would object."

I ask to help in social uplift.

"Why—er—we will write you."

I enter the free field of science. Every laboratory door is closed and no endowments are available.

I seek the universal mistress, Art; the studio door is locked.

I write literature. "We cannot publish stories of colored folks of that type." It's the only type I know.

This is my life. It makes me idiotic. It gives me artificial problems. I hesitate, I rush, I waver. In fine,—I am sensitive!

My pale friend looks at me with disbelief and curling tongue.

"Do you mean to sit there and tell me that this is what happens to you each day?"

Certainly not, I answer low.

"Then you only fear it will happen?"

I fear!

"Well, haven't you the courage to rise above a—almost a craven fear?"

Quite—quite craven is my fear, I admit; but the terrible thing is—these things do happen!

"But you just said——"

They do happen. Not all each day,—surely not. But now and then—now seldom, now, sudden; now after a week, now in a chain of awful minutes; not everywhere, but anywhere—in Boston, in Atlanta. That's the hell of it. Imagine spending your life looking for insults or for hiding places from them—shrinking (instinctively and despite desperate bolsterings of courage) from blows that are not always but ever; not each day, but each week, each month, each year. Just, perhaps, as you have choked back the craven fear and cried, "I am and will be the master of my——"

"No more tickets downstairs; here's one to the smoking gallery."

You hesitate. You beat back your suspicions. After all, a cigarette with Charlie Chaplin—then a white man pushes by—"Three in the orchestra."

"Yes, sir." And in he goes.

Suddenly your heart chills. You turn yourself away toward the golden twinkle of the purple night and hesitate again. What's the use? Why not always yield—always take what's offered,—always bow to force, whether of cannon or dislike? Then the great fear surges in your soul, the real fear—the fear beside which other fears are vain imaginings; the fear lest right there and then you are losing your own soul; that you are losing your own soul and the soul of a people; that millions of unborn children, black and gold and mauve, are being there and then despoiled by you because you are a coward and dare not fight!

Suddenly that silly orchestra seat and the cavorting of a comedian with funny feet become matters of life, death, and immortality; you grasp the pillars of the universe and strain as you sway back to that befrilled ticket girl. You grip your soul for riot and murder. You choke and sputter, and she seeing that you are about to make a "fuss" obeys her orders and throws the tickets at you in contempt. Then you slink to your seat and crouch in the darkness before the film, with every tissue burning! The miserable wave of reaction engulfs you. To think of compelling puppies to take your hard-earned money; fattening hogs to hate you and yours; forcing your way among cheap and tawdry idiots—God! What a night of pleasure!

Here, then, is beauty and ugliness, a wide vision of world-sacrifice, a fierce gleam of world-hate. Which is life and what is death and how shall we face so tantalizing a contradiction? Any explanation must necessarily be subtle and involved. No pert and easy word of encouragement, no merely dark despair, can lay hold of the roots of these things. And first and before all, we cannot forget that this world is beautiful. Grant all its ugliness and sin—the petty, horrible snarl of its putrid threads, which few have seen more near or more often than I—notwithstanding all this, the beauty of this world is not to be denied.

Casting my eyes about I dare not let them rest on the beauty of Love and Friend, for even if my tongue were cunning enough to sing this, the revelation of reality here is too sacred and the fancy too untrue. Of one world-beauty alone may we at once be brutally frank and that is the glory of physical nature; this, though the least of beauties, is divine!

And so, too, there are depths of human degradation which it is not fair for us to probe. With all their horrible prevalence, we cannot call them natural. But may we not compare the least of the world's beauty with the least of its ugliness—not murder, starvation, and rapine, with love and friendship and creation—but the glory of sea and sky and city, with the little hatefulnesses and thoughtlessnesses of race prejudice, that out of such juxtaposition we may, perhaps, deduce some rule of beauty and life—or death?

There mountains hurl themselves against the stars and at their feet lie black and leaden seas. Above float clouds— white, gray, and inken, while the clear, impalpable air springs and sparkles like new wine. Last night we floated on the calm bosom of the sea in the southernmost haven of Mount Desert. The water flamed and sparkled. The sun had gone, but above the crooked back of cumulus clouds, dark and pink with radiance, and on the other sky aloft to the eastward piled the gorgeous-curtained mists of evening. The radiance faded and a shadowy velvet veiled the mountains, a humid depth of gloom behind which lurked all the mysteries of life and death, while above, the clouds hung ashen and dull; lights twinkled and flashed along the shore, boats glided in the twilight, and the little puffing of motors droned away. Then was the hour to talk of life and the meaning of life, while above gleamed silently, suddenly, star on star.

Bar Harbor lies beneath a mighty mountain, a great, bare, black mountain that sleeps above the town; but as you leave, it rises suddenly, threateningly, until far away on Frenchman's Bay it looms above the town in withering vastness, as if to call all that little world petty save itself. Beneath the cool, wide stare of that great mountain, men cannot live as giddily as in some lesser summer's playground. Before the unveiled face of nature, as it lies naked on the Maine coast, rises a certain human awe.

God molded his world largely and mightily off this marvelous coast and meant that in the tired days of life men should come and worship here and renew their spirit. This I have done and turning I go to work again. As we go, ever the mountains of Mount Desert rise and greet us on our going—somber, rock-ribbed and silent, looking unmoved on the moving world, yet conscious of their everlasting strength.

About us beats the sea—the sail-flecked, restless sea, humming its tune about our flying keel, unmindful of the voices of men. The land sinks to meadows, black pine forests, with here and there a blue and wistful mountain. Then there are islands—bold rocks above the sea, curled meadows; through and about them roll ships, weather-beaten and patched of sail, strong-hulled and smoking, light gray and shining. All the colors of the sea lie about us—gray and yellowing greens and doubtful blues, blacks not quite black, tinted silvers and golds and dreaming whites. Long tongues of dark and golden land lick far out into the tossing waters, and the white gulls sail and scream above them. It is a mighty coast—ground out and pounded, scarred, crushed, and carven in massive, frightful lineaments. Everywhere stand the pines—the little dark and steadfast pines that smile not, neither weep, but wait and wait. Near us lie isles of flesh and blood, white cottages, tiled and meadowed. Afar lie shadow-lands, high mist-hidden hills, mountains boldly limned, yet shading to the sky, faint and unreal.

We skirt the pine-clad shores, chary of men, and know how bitterly winter kisses these lonely shores to fill yon row of beaked ice houses that creep up the hills. We are sailing due westward and the sun, yet two hours high, is blazoning a fiery glory on the sea that spreads and gleams like some broad, jeweled trail, to where the blue and distant shadow-land lifts its carven front aloft, leaving, as it gropes, shades of shadows beyond.

Why do not those who are scarred in the world's battle and hurt by its hardness travel to these places of beauty and drown themselves in the utter joy of life? I asked this once sitting in a Southern home. Outside the spring of a Georgia February was luring gold to the bushes and languor to the soft air. Around me sat color in human flesh—brown that crimsoned readily; dim soft-yellow that escaped description; cream-like duskiness that shadowed to rich tints of autumn leaves. And yet a suggested journey in the world brought no response.

"I should think you would like to travel," said the white one.

But no, the thought of a journey seemed to depress them.

Did you ever see a "Jim-Crow" waiting-room? There are always exceptions, as at Greensboro—but usually there is no heat in winter and no air in summer; with undisturbed loafers and train hands and broken, disreputable settees; to buy a ticket is torture; you stand and stand and wait and wait until every white person at the "other window" is waited on. Then the tired agent yells across, because all the tickets and money are over there.

"What d'ye want? What? Where?"

The agent browbeats and contradicts you, hurries and confuses the ignorant, gives many persons the wrong change, compels some to purchase their tickets on the train at a higher price, and sends you and me out on the plat-form, burning with indignation and hatred!

The "Jim-Crow" car is up next the baggage car and engine. It stops out beyond the covering in the rain or sun or dust. Usually there is no step to help you climb on and often the car is a smoker cut in two and you must pass through the white smokers or else they pass through your part, with swagger and noise and stares. Your compartment is a half or a quarter or an eighth of the oldest car in service on the road. Unless it happens to be a through express, the plush is caked with dirt, the floor is grimy, and the windows dirty. An impertinent white newsboy occupies two seats at the end of the car and importunes you to the point of rage to buy cheap candy, Coco-Cola, and worthless, if not vulgar, books. He yells and swaggers, while a continued stream of white men saunters back and forth from the smoker to buy and hear. The white train crew from the baggage car uses the "Jim-Crow" to lounge in and perform their toilet. The conductor appropriates two seats for himself and his papers and yells gruffly for your tickets before the train has scarcely started. It is best not to ask him for information even in the gentlest tones. His information is for white persons chiefly. It is difficult to get lunch or clean water. Lunch rooms either don't serve niggers or serve them at some dirty and ill-attended hole in the wall. As for toilet rooms,—don't! If you have to change cars, be wary of junctions which are usually without accommodation and filled with quarrelsome white persons who hate a "darky dressed up." You are apt to have the company of a sheriff and a couple of meek or sullen black prisoners on part of your way and dirty colored section hands will pour in toward night and drive you to the smallest corner.

"No," said the little lady in the corner (she looked like an ivory cameo and her dress flowed on her like a caress), "We don't travel much."

Pessimism is cowardice. The man who cannot frankly acknowledge the "Jim-Crow" car as a fact and yet live and hope is simply afraid either of himself or of the world. There is not in the world a more disgraceful denial of human brotherhood than the "Jim-Crow" car of the southern United States; but, too, just as true, there is nothing more beautiful in the universe than sunset and moonlight on Montego Bay in far Jamaica. And both things are true and both belong to this our world, and neither can be denied.

The sun, prepared to cross that awful border which men call Night and Death, marshals his hosts. I seem to see the spears of mighty horsemen flash golden in the light; empurpled banners flame afar, and the low thunder of marching hosts thrills with the thunder of the sea. Athwart his own path, screening a face of fire, he throws cloud masses, masking his trained guns. And then the miracle is done. The host passes with roar too vast for human ear and the sun is set, leaving the frightened moon and blinded stars.

In the dusk the green-gold palms turn their starlike faces and stretch their fan-like fingers, lifting themselves proudly, lest any lordly leaf should know the taint of earth.

Out from the isle the serpent hill thrusts its great length around the bay, shouldering back the waters and the shadows. Ghost rains sweep down, smearing his rugged sides, yet on he writhes, undulant with pine and palm, gleaming until his low, sharp head and lambent tongue, grown gray and pale and silver in the dying day, kisses the molten gold of the golden sea.

Then comes the moon. Like fireflies nesting in the hand of God gleams the city, dim-swathed by fairy palms. A long, thin thumb, mist-mighty, points shadowy to the Spanish

Main, while through the fingers foam the Seven Seas.
Above the calm and gold-green moon, beneath the wind-
wet earth; and here, alone, my soul enchained, enchanted!

From such heights of holiness men turn to master the
world. All the pettiness of life drops away and it becomes a
great battle before the Lord. His trumpet,—where does it
sound and whither? I go. I saw Montego Bay at the beginning of the World War. The cry for service as high as
heaven, as wide as human feeling, seemed filling the earth.
What were petty slights, silly insults, paltry problems, beside
this call to do and dare and die? We black folk offered our
services to fight. What happened? Most Americans have
forgotten the extraordinary series of events which worked
the feelings of black America to fever heat.

First was the refusal to accept Negro volunteers for the
army, except in the four black regiments already established.
While the nation was combing the country for volunteers
for the regular army, it would not let the American Negro
furnish even his proportionate quota of regular soldiers.
This led to some grim bantering among Negroes:

"Why do you want to volunteer?" asked many. "Why
should you fight for this country?"

Before we had chance to reply to this, there came the
army draft bill and the proposal by Vardaman and his ilk to
except Negroes. We protested to Washington in various
ways, and while we were insisting that colored men should
be drafted just as other citizens, the bill went through with
two little "jokers."

First, it provided that Negroes should be drafted, but
trained in "separate" units; and, secondly, it somewhat
ambiguously permitted men to be drafted for "labor."

A wave of fear and unrest spread among Negroes and

while we were looking at both these provisions askance, suddenly we received the draft registration blank. It directed persons "of African descent" to "tear off the corner!" Probably never before in the history of the United States has a portion of the citizens been so openly and crassly discriminated against by action of the general government. It was disheartening, and on top of it came the celebrated "German plots." It was alleged in various parts of the country with singular unanimity that Germans were working among the Negroes, and it was further intimated that this would make the Negroes too dangerous an element to trust with guns. To us, of course, it looked as though the discovery and the proposition came from the same thinly-veiled sources.

Considering carefully this series of happenings the American Negro sensed an approaching crisis and faced a puzzling dilemma. Here was evidently preparing fertile ground for the spread of disloyalty and resentment among the black masses, as they were forced to choose apparently between forced labor or a "Jim-Crow" draft. Manifestly when a minority group is thus segregated and forced out of the nation, they can in reason do but one thing—take advantage of the disadvantage. In this case we demanded colored officers for the colored troops.

General Wood was early approached and asked to admit suitable candidates to Plattsburg. He refused. We thereupon pressed the government for a "separate" camp for the training of Negro officers. Not only did the War Department hesitate at this request, but strong opposition arose among colored people themselves. They said we were going too far. "We will obey the law, but to ask for voluntary segregation is to insult ourselves." But strong, sober second thought came to our rescue. We said to our protesting brothers: "We face a condition, not a theory. There is not the slightest chance of our being admitted to white camps; therefore, it is either a case of a 'Jim-Crow' officers' training camp or no colored officers. Of the two things no colored officers would be the greater calamity."

Thus we gradually made up our minds. But the War Department still hesitated. It was besieged, and when it presented its final argument, "We have no place for such a camp," the trustees of Howard University said: "Take our campus." Eventually twelve hundred colored cadets were assembled at Fort Des Moines for officers' training.

The city of Des Moines promptly protested, but it finally changed its mind. Des Moines never before had seen such a class of colored men. They rapidly became popular with all classes and many encomiums were passed upon their conduct. Their commanding colonel pronounced their work first class and declared that they presented excellent material for officers.

Meantime, with one accord, the thought of the colored people turned toward Colonel Young, their highest officer in the regular army. Charles Young is a heroic figure. He is the typical soldier,—silent, uncomplaining, brave, and efficient! From his days at West Point throughout his thirty years of service he has taken whatever task was assigned him and performed it efficiently; and there is no doubt but that the army has been almost merciless in the requirements which it has put upon this splendid officer. He came through all with flying colors. In Haiti, in Liberia, in western camps, in the Sequoia Forests of California, and finally with Pershing in Mexico,—in every case he triumphed. Just at the time we were looking to the United States government to call him to head the colored officers' training at Des Moines, he was retired from the army, because of "high blood pressure!" There is no disputing army surgeons and their judgment in this case may be justified, but coming at the time it did, nearly every Negro in the United States believed that the "high blood pressure" that retired Colonel Young was in the prejudiced heads of the Southern oligarchy who were determined that no American Negro should ever wear the stars of a General.

To say that Negroes of the United States were disheartened at the retirement of Colonel Young is to put it mildly,—but there was more trouble. The provision that Negroes must be trained separately looked simple and was simple in places where there were large Negro contingents, but in the North with solitary Negroes drafted here and there we had some extraordinary developments. Regiments appeared with one Negro where the Negro had to be separated like a pest and put into a house or even a village by himself while the commander frantically telegraphed to Washington. Small wonder that one poor fellow in Ohio solved the problem by cutting his throat. The whole process of drafting Negroes had to be held up until the government could find methods and places for assembling them.

Then came Houston. In a moment the nation forgot the whole record of one of the most celebrated regiments in the United States Army and its splendid service in the Indian Wars and in the Philippines. It was the first regiment mobilized in the Spanish-American War and it was the regiment that volunteered to a man to clean up the yellow fever camps when others hesitated. It was one of the regiments to which Pershing said in December:

"Men, I am authorized by Congress to tell you all that our people back in the States are mightily glad and proud at the way the soldiers have conducted themselves while in Mexico, and I, General Pershing, can say with pride that a finer body of men never stood under the flag of our nation than we find here tonight."

The nation, also, forgot the deep resentment mixed with the pale ghost of fear which Negro soldiers call up in the breasts of the white South. It is not so much that they fear that the Negro will strike if he gets a chance, but rather that they assume with curious unanimity that he has *reason* to strike, that any other persons in his circumstances or treated as he is would rebel. Instead of seeking to relieve the cause of such a possible feeling, most of them strain every effort to bottle up the black man's resentment. Is it inconceivable that now and then it bursts all bounds, as at Brownsville and Houston?

So in the midst of this mental turmoil came Houston and East St. Louis. At Houston black soldiers, goaded and insulted, suddenly went wild and "shot up" the town. At East St. Louis white strikers on war work killed and mobbed Negro workingmen, and as a result 19 colored soldiers were hanged and 51 imprisoned for life for killing 17 whites at Houston, while for killing 125 Negroes in East St. Louis, 20 white men were imprisoned, none for more than 15 years, and 10 colored men with them.

Once upon a time I took a great journey in this land to three of the ends of our world and over seven thousand mighty miles. I saw the grim desert and the high ramparts of the Rocky Mountains. Three days I flew from the silver beauty of Seattle to the somber whirl of Kansas City. Three days I flew from the brute might of Chicago to the air of the Angels in California, scented with golden flowers, where the homes of men crouch low and loving on the good, broad earth, as though they were kissing her blossoms. Three days I flew through the empire of Texas, but all these shall be tales untold, for in all this journey I saw but one thing that lived and will live eternal in my soul,—the Grand Cañon.

It is a sudden void in the bosom of earth, down to its entrails—a wound where the dull titanic knife has turned and twisted in the hole, leaving its edges livid, scarred, jagged, and pulsing over the white, and red, and purple of its mighty flesh, while down below—down, down below, in black and severed vein, boils the dull and sullen flood of the Colorado.

It is awful. There can be nothing like it. It is the earth and sky gone stark and raving mad. The mountains up-twirled, disbodied and inverted, stand on their peaks and throw their bowels to the sky. Their earth is air; their ether blood-red rock engreened. You stand upon their roots and fall into their pinnacles, a mighty mile.

Behold this mauve and purple mocking of time and space! See yonder peak! No human foot has trod it. Into that blue shadow only the eye of God has looked. Listen to the accents of that gorge which mutters: "Before Abraham was, I am." Is yonder wall a hedge of black or is it the rampart between heaven and hell? I see greens,—is it moss or giant pines? I see specks that may be boulders. Ever the winds sigh and drop into those sun-swept silences. Ever the gorge lies motionless, unmoved, until I fear. It is a grim thing, unholy, terrible! It is human—some mighty drama unseen, unheard, is playing there its tragedies or mocking comedy, and the laugh of endless years is shrieking onward from peak to peak, unheard, unechoed, and unknown.

One throws a rock into the abyss. It gives back no sound. It falls on silence—the voice of its thunders cannot reach so far. It is not—it cannot be a mere, inert, unfeeling, brute fact—its grandeur is too serene—its beauty too divine! It is not red, and blue, and green, but, ah! the shadows and the shades of all the world, glad colorings touched with a hesitant spiritual delicacy. What does it mean—what does it mean? Tell me, black and boiling water!

It is not real. It is but shadows. The shading of eternity. Last night yonder tesselated palace was gloom—dark, brooding thought and sin, while hither rose the mountains of the sun, golden, blazing, ensanguined. It was a dream. This blue and brilliant morning shows all those burning peaks alight, while here, shapeless, mistful, brood the shadowed towers.

I have been down into the entrails of earth—down, down by straight and staring cliffs—down by sounding waters and sun-strewn meadows; down by green pastures and still waters, by great, steep chasms—down by the gnarled and twisted fists of God to the deep, sad moan of the yellow river that did this thing of wonder,—a little winding river with death in its depth and a crown of glory in its flying hair.

I have seen what eye of man was never meant to see. I have profaned the sanctuary. I have looked upon the dread disrobing of the Night, and yet I live. Ere I hid my head she was standing in her cavern halls, glowing coldly westward— her feet were blackness: her robes, empurpled, flowed mistily from shoulder down in formless folds of folds; her head, pine-crowned, was set with jeweled stars. I turned away and dreamed—the cañon,—the awful, its depths called; its heights shuddered. Then suddenly I arose and looked. Her robes were falling. At dim-dawn they hung purplish-green and black. Slowly she stripped them from her gaunt and shapely limbs—her cold, gray garments shot with shadows stood revealed. Down dropped the black-blue robes, gray-pearled, and slipped, leaving a filmy, silken, misty thing, and underneath I glimpsed her limbs of utter light.

My God! For what am I thankful this night? For
nothing. For nothing but the most commonplace of com-
monplaces; a table of gentlewomen and gentlemen—soft-
spoken, sweet-tempered, full of human sympathy, who
made me, a stranger, one of them. Ours was a fellowship of
common books, common knowledge, mighty aims. We
could laugh and joke and think as friends—and the
Thing—the hateful, murderous, dirty Thing which in
America we call "Nigger-hatred" was not only not there—
it could not even be understood. It was a curious mon-
strosity at which civilized folk laughed or looked puzzled.
There was no elegant and elaborate condescension of—"We
once had a colored servant"—"My father was an Abolition-
ist"—"I've always been interested in *your people*"—there was
only the community of kindred souls, the delicate reverence
for the Thought that led, the quick deference to the guest.
You left in quiet regret, knowing that they were not dis-
cussing you behind your back with lies and license. God! It
was simply human decency and I had to be thankful for it
because I am an American Negro, and white America, with
saving exceptions, is cruel to everything that has black
blood—and this was Paris, in the years of salvation, 1919.
Fellow blacks, we must join the democracy of Europe.

Toul! Dim through the deepening dark of early after-
noon, I saw its towers gloom dusky toward the murk of
heaven. We wound in misty roads and dropped upon the city
through the great throats of its walled bastions. There lay
France—a strange, unknown, unfamiliar France. The city
was dispossessed. Through its streets—its narrow, winding
streets, old and low and dark, carven and quaint,—poured
thousands upon thousands of strange feet of khaki-clad for-
eigners, and the echoes threw back awkward syllables that

were never French. Here was France beaten to her knees yet fighting as never nation fought before, calling in her death agony across the seas till her help came and with all its strut and careless braggadocio saved the worthiest nation of the world from the wickedest fate ever plotted by Fools.

Tim Brimm was playing by the town-pump. Tim Brimm and the bugles of Harlem blared in the little streets of Maron in far Lorraine. The tiny streets were seas of mud. Dank mist and rain sifted through the cold air above the blue Moselle. Soldiers—soldiers everywhere—black soldiers, boys of Washington, Alabama, Philadelphia, Mississippi. Wild and sweet and wooing leapt the strains upon the air. French children gazed in wonder—women left their washing. Up in the window stood a black Major, a Captain, a Teacher, and I—with tears behind our smiling eyes. Tim Brimm was playing by the town-pump.

The audience was framed in smoke. It rose ghost-like out of memories—bitter memories of the officer near dead of pneumonia whose pain was lighted up by the nurses waiting to know whether he must be "Jim-Crowed" with privates or not. Memories of that great last morning when the thunders of hell called the Ninety-second to its last drive. Memories of bitter humiliations, determined triumphs, great victories, and bugle-calls that sounded from earth to heaven. Like memories framed in the breath of God, my audience peered in upon me—good, brown faces with great, kind, beautiful eyes—black soldiers of America rescuing beloved France—and the words came in praise and benediction there in the "Y," with its little stock of cigarettes and candies and its rusty wood stove.

"*Alors*," said Madame, "*quatre sont morts*"—four dead— four tall, strong sons dead for France—sons like the sweet and blue-eyed daughter who was hiding her brave smile in the dusk. It was a tiny stone house whose front window lipped the passing sidewalk where ever tramped the feet of black soldiers marching home. There was a cavernous wardrobe, a great fireplace invaded by a new and jaunty iron stove. Vast, thick piles of bedding rose in yonder corner. Without was the crowded kitchen and up a half-stair was our bedroom that gave upon a tiny court with arched stone staircase and one green tree. We were a touching family party held together by a great sorrow and a great joy. How we laughed over the salad that got brandy instead of vinegar—how we ate the golden pile of fried potatoes and how we pored over the post-card from the Lieutenant of the Senegalese—dear little vale of crushed and risen France, in the day when Negroes went "over the top" at Pont-à-Mousson.

Paris, Paris by purple façade of the opera, the crowd on the Boulevard des Italiens and the great swing of the Champs Elysées. But not the Paris the world knows. Paris with its soul cut to the core—feverish, crowded, nervous, hurried; full of uniforms and mourning bands, with cafés closed at 9:30—no sugar, scarce bread, and tears so interwined with joy that there is scant difference. Paris has been dreaming a nightmare, and though she awakes, the grim terror is upon her—it lies on the sand-closed art treasures of the Louvre. Only the flowers are there, always the flowers, the Roses of England and the Lilies of France.

New York! Behind the Liberty that faces free France rise the white cliffs of Manhattan, tier on tier, with a curving pinnacle, towers square and twin, a giant inkwell daintily stoppered, an ancient pyramid enthroned; beneath, low ramparts wide and mighty; while above, faint-limned against the turbulent sky, looms the vast grace of that Cathedral of the Purchased and Purchasing Poor, topping the world and pointing higher.

Yonder the gray cobwebs of the Brooklyn bridges leap the sea, and here creep the argosies from all earth's ends. We move to this swift home on dun and swelling waters and hear as we come the heartbeats of the new world.

New York and night from the Brooklyn Bridge: The bees and fireflies flit and twinkle in their vast hives; curved clouds like the breath of gods hover between the towers and the moon. One hears the hiss of lightnings, the deep thunder of human things, and a fevered breathing as of some attendant and invincible Powers. The glow of burning millions melts outward into dim and fairy outlines until afar the liquid music born of rushing crowds drips like a benediction on the sea.

New York and morning: the sun is kissing the timid dew in Central Park, and from the Fountain of Plenty one looks along that world street, Fifth Avenue, and walks toward town. The earth lifts and curves graciously down from the older mansions of princes to the newer shops of luxury. Egypt and Abyssinia, Paris and Damascus, London and India caress you by the way; churches stand aloof while the shops swell to emporiums. But all this is nothing. Everything is mankind. Humanity stands and flies and walks and rolls about—the poor, the priceless, the world-known and the forgotten; child and grandfather, king and leman—the pageant of the world goes by, set in a frame of stone and jewels, clothed in scarlet and rags. Princes Street and the Elysian Fields, the Strand and the Ringstrasse—these are the Ways of the World today.

New York and twilight, there where the Sixth Avenue "L" rises and leaps above the tenements into the free air at 110th Street. It circles like a bird with heaven and St. John's above and earth and the sweet green and gold of the Park beneath. Beyond lie all the blue mists and mysteries of distance; beneath, the city rushes and crawls. Behind echo all the roar and war and care and maze of the wide city set in its sullen darkening walls, flashing weird and crimson farewells. Out at the sides the stars twinkle.

Again New York and Night and Harlem. A dark city of fifty thousand rises like magic from the earth. Gone is the white world, the pale lips, the lank hair; gone is the West and North—the East and South is here triumphant. The street is crowd and leisure and laughter. Everywhere black eyes, black and brown, and frizzled hair curled and sleek, and skins that riot with luscious color and deep, burning blood. Humanity is packed dense in high piles of close-knit homes that lie in layers above gray shops of food and clothes and drink, with here and there a moving-picture show. Orators declaim on the corners, lovers lark in the streets, gamblers glide by the saloons, workers lounge wearily home. Children scream and run and frolic, and all is good and human and beautiful and ugly and evil, even as Life is elsewhere.

And then—the Veil. It drops as drops the night on southern seas—vast, sudden, unanswering. There is Hate behind it, and Cruelty and Tears. As one peers through its intricate, unfathomable pattern of ancient, old, old design, one sees blood and guilt and misunderstanding. And yet it hangs there, this Veil, between Then and Now, between Pale and Colored and Black and White—between You and

Me. Surely it is a thought-thing, tenuous, intangible; yet just as surely is it true and terrible and not in our little day may you and I lift it. We may feverishly unravel its edges and even climb slow with giant shears to where its ringed and gilded top nestles close to the throne of God. But as we work and climb we shall see through streaming eyes and hear with aching ears, lynching and murder, cheating and despising, degrading and lying, so flashed and fleshed through this vast hanging darkness that the Doer never sees the Deed and the Victim knows not the Victor and Each hates All in wild and bitter ignorance. Listen, O Isles, to these Voices from within the Veil, for they portray the most human hurt of the Twentieth Cycle of that poor Jesus who was called the Christ!

There is something in the nature of Beauty that demands an end. Ugliness may be indefinite. It may trail off into gray endlessness. But Beauty must be complete—whether it be a field of poppies or a great life,—it must end, and the End is part and triumph of the Beauty. I know there are those who envisage a beauty eternal. But I cannot. I can dream of great and never-ending processions of beautiful things and visions and acts. But each must be complete or it cannot for me exist.

On the other hand, Ugliness to me is eternal, not in the essence but in its incompleteness; but its eternity does not daunt me, for its eternal unfulfilment is a cause of joy. There is in it nothing new or unexpected; it is the old evil stretching out and ever seeking the end it cannot find; it may coil and writhe and recur in endless battle to days without end, but it is the same human ill and bitter hurt. But Beauty is fulfilment. It satisfies. It is always new and strange. It is the reasonable thing. Its end is Death—the sweet silence of perfection, the calm and balance of utter music. Therein is the triumph of Beauty.

So strong is the spell of beauty that there are those who, contradicting their own knowledge and experience, try to say that all is beauty. They are called optimists, and they lie. All is not beauty. Ugliness and hate and ill are here with all their contradiction and illogic; they will always be here—perhaps, God send, with lessened volume and force, but here and eternal, while beauty triumphs in its great completion—Death. We cannot conjure the end of all ugliness in eternal beauty, for beauty by its very being and definition has in each definition its ends and limits; but while beauty lies implicit and revealed in its end, ugliness writhes on in darkness forever. So the ugliness of continual birth fulfils itself and conquers gloriously only in the beautiful end, Death.

At last to us all comes happiness, there in the Court of Peace, where the dead lie so still and calm and good. If we were not dead we would lie and listen to the flowers grow. We would hear the birds sing and see how the rain rises and blushes and burns and pales and dies in beauty. We would see spring, summer, and the red riot of autumn, and then in winter, beneath the soft white snow, sleep and dream of dreams. But we know that being dead, our Happiness is a fine and finished thing and that ten, a hundred, and a thousand years, we shall lie at rest, unhurt in the Court of Peace.

The Prayers of God

Name of God's Name!
Red murder reigns;
All hell is loose;
On gold autumnal air
Walk grinning devils, barbed and hoofed;
While high on hills of hate,
Black-blossomed, crimson-sky'd,
Thou sittest, dumb.

Father Almighty!
This earth is mad!
Palsied, our cunning hands;
Rotten, our gold;
Our argosies reel and stagger
Over empty seas;
All the long aisles
Of Thy Great Temples, God,
Stink with the entrails
Of our souls.
And Thou art dumb.

Above the thunder of Thy Thunders, Lord,
Lightening Thy Lightnings,
Rings and roars
The dark damnation

Of this hell of war.
Red piles the pulp of hearts and heads
And little children's hands.

Allah!
Elohim!
Very God of God!
Death is here!
Dead are the living; deep-dead the dead.
Dying are earth's unborn—
The babes' wide eyes of genius and of joy,
Poems and prayers, sun-glows and earth-songs,
Great-pictured dreams,
Enmarbled phantasies,
High hymning heavens—all
In this dread night
Writhe and shriek and choke and die
This long ghost-night—
While Thou art dumb.

Have mercy!
Have mercy upon us, miserable sinners!
Stand forth, unveil Thy Face,
Pour down the light
That seethes above Thy Throne,
And blaze this devil's dance to darkness!
Hear!
Speak!
In Christ's Great Name—

I hear!
Forgive me, God!
Above the thunder I hearkened;

Beneath the silence, now,—
I hear!

(Wait, God, a little space.
It is so strange to talk with Thee—
Alone!)

This gold?
I took it.
Is it Thine?
Forgive; I did not know.
Blood? Is it wet with blood?
'Tis from my brother's hands.
(I know; his hands are mine.)
It flowed for Thee, O Lord.

War? Not so; not war—
Dominion, Lord, and over black, not white;
Black, brown, and fawn,
And not Thy Chosen Brood, O God,
We murdered.
To build Thy Kingdom,
To drape our wives and little ones,
And set their souls a-glitter—
For this we killed these lesser breeds
And civilized their dead,
Raping red rubber, diamonds, cocoa, gold!

For this, too, once, and in Thy Name,
I lynched a Nigger—

    (He raved and writhed,
    I heard him cry,

I felt the life-light leap and lie,
I saw him crackle there, on high,
I watched him wither!)

Thou?
Thee?
I lynched Thee?

Awake me, God! I sleep!
What was that awful word Thou saidst?
That black and riven thing—was it Thee?
That gasp—was it Thine?
This pain—is it Thine?
Are, then, these bullets piercing Thee?
Have all the wars of all the world,
Down all dim time, drawn blood from Thee?
Have all the lies and thefts and hates—
Is this Thy Crucifixion, God,
And not that funny, little cross,
With vinegar and thorns?
Is this Thy kingdom here, not there,
This stone and stucco drift of dreams?

Help!
I sense that low and awful cry—
Who cries?
Who weeps?
With silent sob that rends and tears—
Can God sob?

Who prays?
I hear strong prayers throng by,
Like mighty winds on dusky moors—
Can God pray?

Prayest Thou, Lord, and to me?
Thou needest me?
Thou *needest* me?
Thou needest *me?*
Poor, wounded soul!
Of this I never dreamed. I thought—

Courage, God,
I come!

X | THE COMET

HE stood a moment on the steps of the bank, watching the human river that swirled down Broadway. Few noticed him. Few ever noticed him save in a way that stung. He was outside the world—"nothing!" as he said bitterly. Bits of the words of the walkers came to him.

"The comet?"

"The comet—"

Everybody was talking of it. Even the president, as he entered, smiled patronizingly at him, and asked:

"Well, Jim, are you scared?"

"No," said the messenger shortly.

"I thought we'd journeyed through the comet's tail once," broke in the junior clerk affably.

"Oh, that was Halley's," said the president; "this is a new comet, quite a stranger, they say—wonderful, wonderful! I saw it last night. Oh, by the way, Jim," turning again to the messenger, "I want you to go down into the lower vaults today."

The messenger followed the president silently. Of

course, they wanted *him* to go down to the lower vaults. It was too dangerous for more valuable men. He smiled grimly and listened.

"Everything of value has been moved out since the water began to seep in," said the president; "but we miss two volumes of old records. Suppose you nose around down there,—it isn't very pleasant, I suppose."

"Not very," said the messenger, as he walked out.

"Well, Jim, the tail of the new comet hits us at noon this time," said the vault clerk, as he passed over the keys; but the messenger passed silently down the stairs. Down he went beneath Broadway, where the dim light filtered through the feet of hurrying men; down to the dark basement beneath; down into the blackness and silence beneath that lowest cavern. Here with his dark lantern he groped in the bowels of the earth, under the world.

He drew a long breath as he threw back the last great iron door and stepped into the fetid slime within. Here at last was peace, and he groped moodily forward. A great rat leaped past him and cobwebs crept across his face. He felt carefully around the room, shelf by shelf, on the muddied floor, and in crevice and corner. Nothing. Then he went back to the far end, where somehow the wall felt different. He sounded and pushed and pried. Nothing. He started away. Then something brought him back. He was sounding and working again when suddenly the whole black wall swung as on mighty hinges, and blackness yawned beyond. He peered in; it was evidently a secret vault—some hiding place of the old bank unknown in newer times. He entered hesitatingly. It was a long, narrow room with shelves, and at the far end, an old iron chest. On a high shelf lay the two missing volumes of records, and others. He put them carefully aside and stepped to the chest. It was old, strong, and rusty. He looked at the vast and old-fashioned lock and flashed his light on the hinges. They were deeply incrusted with rust. Looking about, he found a bit of iron and began to pry. The rust had eaten a hundred years, and it had gone deep. Slowly, wearily, the old lid lifted, and with a last, low groan lay bare its treasure—and he saw the dull sheen of gold!

"Boom!"

A low, grinding, reverberating crash struck upon his ear. He started up and looked about. All was black and still. He groped for his light and swung it about him. Then he knew! The great stone door had swung to. He forgot the gold and looked death squarely in the face. Then with a sigh he went methodically to work. The cold sweat stood on his forehead; but he searched, pounded, pushed, and worked until after what seemed endless hours his hand struck a cold bit of metal and the great door swung again harshly on its hinges, and then, striking against something soft and heavy, stopped. He had just room to squeeze through. There lay the body of the vault clerk, cold and stiff. He stared at it, and then felt sick and nauseated. The air seemed unaccountably foul, with a strong, peculiar odor. He stepped forward, clutched at the air, and fell fainting across the corpse.

He awoke with a sense of horror, leaped from the body, and groped up the stairs, calling to the guard. The watchman sat as if asleep, with the gate swinging free. With one glance at him the messenger hurried up to the sub-vault. In vain he called to the guards. His voice echoed and re-echoed weirdly. Up into the great basement he rushed. Here another guard lay prostrate on his face, cold and still. A fear arose in the messenger's heart. He dashed up to the cellar floor, up into the bank. The stillness of death lay everywhere and everywhere bowed, bent, and stretched the silent forms of men. The messenger paused and glanced about. He was not a man easily moved; but the sight was appalling! "Robbery and murder," he whispered slowly to himself as he saw the twisted, oozing mouth of the president where he lay half-buried on his desk. Then a new thought seized him: If they found him here alone—with all this money and all these dead men—what would his life be worth? He glanced about, tiptoed cautiously to a side door, and again looked behind. Quietly he turned the latch and stepped out into Wall Street.

How silent the street was! Not a soul was stirring, and yet it was high-noon—Wall Street? Broadway? He glanced almost wildly up and down, then across the street, and as he looked, a sickening horror froze in his limbs. With a choking cry of utter fright he lunged, leaned giddily against the cold building, and stared helplessly at the sight.

In the great stone doorway a hundred men and women and children lay crushed and twisted and jammed, forced into that great, gaping doorway like refuse in a can—as if in one wild, frantic rush to safety, they had crushed and ground themselves to death. Slowly the messenger crept along the walls, wetting his parched mouth and trying to comprehend, stilling the tremor in his limbs and the rising terror in his heart. He met a business man, silk-hatted and frock-coated, who had crept, too, along that smooth wall and stood now stone dead with wonder written on his lips. The messenger turned his eyes hastily away and sought the curb. A woman leaned wearily against the signpost, her head bowed motionless on her lace and silken bosom. Before her stood a street car, silent, and within—but the messenger but glanced and hurried on. A grimy newsboy sat in the gutter with the "last edition" in his uplifted hand: "Danger!" screamed its black headlines. "Warnings wired around the world. The Comet's tail sweeps past us at noon.

Deadly gases expected. Close doors and windows. Seek the cellar." The messenger read and staggered on. Far out from a window above, a girl lay with gasping face and sleevelets on her arms. On a store step sat a little, sweet-faced girl looking upward toward the skies, and in the carriage by her lay—but the messenger looked no longer. The cords gave way—the terror burst in his veins, and with one great, gasping cry he sprang desperately forward and ran,—ran as only the frightened run, shrieking and fighting the air until with one last wail of pain he sank on the grass of Madison Square and lay prone and still.

When he arose, he gave no glance at the still and silent forms on the benches, but, going to a fountain, bathed his face; then hiding himself in a corner away from the drama of death, he quietly gripped himself and thought the thing through: The comet had swept the earth and this was the end. Was everybody dead? He must search and see.

He knew that he must steady himself and keep calm, or he would go insane. First he must go to a restaurant. He walked up Fifth Avenue to a famous hostelry and entered its gorgeous, ghost-haunted halls. He beat back the nausea, and, seizing a tray from dead hands, hurried into the street and ate ravenously, hiding to keep out the sights.

"Yesterday, they would not have served me," he whispered, as he forced the food down.

Then he started up the street,—looking, peering, telephoning, ringing alarms; silent, silent all. Was nobody—nobody—he dared not think the thought and hurried on.

Suddenly he stopped still. He had forgotten. My God! How could he have forgotten? He must rush to the subway—then he almost laughed. No—a car; if he could find a Ford. He saw one. Gently he lifted off its burden, and took his place on the seat. He tested the throttle. There was

gas. He glided off, shivering, and drove up the street. Everywhere stood, leaned, lounged, and lay the dead, in grim and
awful silence. On he ran past an automobile, wrecked and
overturned; past another, filled with a gay party whose
smiles yet lingered on their death-struck lips; on past crowds
and groups of cars, pausing by dead policemen; at 42nd
Street he had to detour to Park Avenue to avoid the dead
congestion. He came back on Fifth Avenue at 57th and flew
past the Plaza and by the park with its hushed babies and
silent throng, until as he was rushing past 72nd Street he
heard a sharp cry, and saw a living form leaning wildly out
an upper window. He gasped. The human voice sounded in
his ears like the voice of God.

"Hello—hello—help, in God's name!" wailed the
woman. "There's a dead girl in here and a man and—and
see yonder dead men lying in the street and dead horses—
for the love of God go and bring the officers——" And the
words trailed off into hysterical tears.

He wheeled the car in a sudden circle, running over the
still body of a child and leaping on the curb. Then he
rushed up the steps and tried the door and rang violently.
There was a long pause, but at last the heavy door swung
back. They stared a moment in silence. She had not noticed
before that he was a Negro. He had not thought of her as
white. She was a woman of perhaps twenty-five—rarely
beautiful and richly gowned, with darkly-golden hair, and
jewels. Yesterday, he thought with bitterness, she would
scarcely have looked at him twice. He would have been dirt
beneath her silken feet. She stared at him. Of all the sorts of
men she had pictured as coming to her rescue she had not
dreamed of one like him. Not that he was not human, but
he dwelt in a world so far from hers, so infinitely far, that
he seldom even entered her thought. Yet as she looked at

him curiously he seemed quite commonplace and usual. He was a tall, dark workingman of the better class, with a sensitive face trained to stolidity and a poor man's clothes and hands. His face was soft and slow and his manner at once cold and nervous, like fires long banked, but not out.

So a moment each paused and gauged the other; then the thought of the dead world without rushed in and they started toward each other.

"What has happened?" she cried. "Tell me! Nothing stirs. All is silence! I see the dead strewn before my window as winnowed by the breath of God,—and see——" She dragged him through great, silken hangings to where, beneath the sheen of mahogany and silver, a little French maid lay stretched in quiet, everlasting sleep, and near her a butler lay prone in his livery.

The tears streamed down the woman's cheeks and she clung to his arm until the perfume of her breath swept his face and he felt the tremors racing through her body.

"I had been shut up in my dark room developing pictures of the comet which I took last night; when I came out—I saw the dead!

"What has happened?" she cried again.

He answered slowly:

"Something—comet or devil—swept across the earth this morning and—many are dead!"

"Many? Very many?"

"I have searched and I have seen no other living soul but you."

She gasped and they stared at each other.

"My—father!" she whispered.

"Where is he?"

"He started for the office."

"Where is it?"

"In the Metropolitan Tower."

"Leave a note for him here and come."

Then he stopped.

"No," he said firmly—"first, we must go—to Harlem."

"Harlem!" she cried. Then she understood. She tapped her foot at first impatiently. She looked back and shuddered. Then she came resolutely down the steps.

"There's a swifter car in the garage in the court," she said.

"I don't know how to drive it," he said.

"I do," she answered.

In ten minutes they were flying to Harlem on the wind. The Stutz rose and raced like an airplane. They took the turn at 110th Street on two wheels and slipped with a shriek into 135th.

He was gone but a moment. Then he returned, and his face was gray. She did not look, but said:

"You have lost—somebody?"

"I have lost—everybody," he said, simply—"unless——"

He ran back and was gone several minutes—hours they seemed to her.

"Everybody," he said, and he walked slowly back with something film-like in his hand which he stuffed into his pocket.

"I'm afraid I was selfish," he said. But already the car was moving toward the park among the dark and lined dead of Harlem—the brown, still faces, the knotted hands, the homely garments, and the silence—the wild and haunting silence. Out of the park, and down Fifth Avenue they whirled. In and out among the dead they slipped and quivered, needing no sound of bell or horn, until the great, square Metropolitan Tower hove in sight. Gently he laid the dead elevator boy aside; the car shot upward. The door of the office stood open. On the threshold lay the stenographer, and, staring at her, sat the dead clerk. The inner office was empty, but a note lay on the desk, folded and addressed but unsent:

Dear Daughter:
I've gone for a hundred mile spin in Fred's new Mercedes. Shall not be back before dinner. I'll bring Fred with me.

J.B.H.

"Come," she cried nervously. "We must search the city."

Up and down, over and across, back again—on went that ghostly search. Everywhere was silence and death—death and silence! They hunted from Madison Square to Spuyten Duyvel; they rushed across the Williamsburg Bridge; they swept over Brooklyn; from the Battery and Morningside Heights they scanned the river. Silence, silence everywhere, and no human sign. Haggard and bedraggled they puffed a third time slowly down Broadway, under the broiling sun, and at last stopped. He sniffed the air. An odor—a smell—and with the shifting breeze a sickening stench filled their nostrils and brought its awful warning. The girl settled back helplessly in her seat.

"What can we do?" she cried.

It was his turn now to take the lead, and he did it quickly.

"The long distance telephone—the telegraph and the cable—night rockets and then—flight!"

She looked at him now with strength and confidence. He did not look like men, as she had always pictured men; but he acted like one and she was content. In fifteen minutes they were at the central telephone exchange. As they

came to the door he stepped quickly before her and pressed
her gently back as he closed it. She heard him moving to
and fro, and knew his burdens—the poor, little burdens he
bore. When she entered, he was alone in the room. The
grim switchboard flashed its metallic face in cryptic, sphinx-
like immobility. She seated herself on a stool and donned
the bright earpiece. She looked at the mouthpiece. She had
never looked at one so closely before. It was wide and black,
pimpled with usage; inert; dead; almost sarcastic in its
unfeeling curves. It looked—she beat back the thought—
but it looked,—it persisted in looking like—she turned her
head and found herself alone. One moment she was terri-
fied; then she thanked him silently for his delicacy and
turned resolutely, with a quick intaking of breath.

"Hello!" she called in low tones. She was calling to the
world. The world *must* answer. Would the world *answer*?
Was the world—

Silence!

She had spoken too low.

"Hello!" she cried, full-voiced.

She listened. Silence! Her heart beat quickly. She cried
in clear, distinct, loud tones: "Hello—hello—hello!"

What was that whirring? Surely—no—was it the click
of a receiver?

She bent close, she moved the pegs in the holes, and
called and called, until her voice rose almost to a shriek, and
her heart hammered. It was as if she had heard the last
flicker of creation, and the evil was silence. Her voice
dropped to a sob. She sat stupidly staring into the black and
sarcastic mouthpiece, and the thought came again. Hope lay
dead within her. Yes, the cable and the rockets remained;
but the world—she could not frame the thought or say the
word. It was too mighty—too terrible! She turned toward

the door with a new fear in her heart. For the first time she seemed to realize that she was alone in the world with a stranger, with something more than a stranger,—with a man alien in blood and culture—unknown, perhaps unknowable. It was awful! She must escape—she must fly; he must not see her again. Who knew what awful thoughts—

She gathered her silken skirts deftly about her young, smooth limbs—listened, and glided into a side-hall. A moment she shrank back: the hall lay filled with dead women; then she leaped to the door and tore at it, with bleeding fingers, until it swung wide. She looked out. He was standing at the top of the alley,—silhouetted, tall and black, motionless. Was he looking at her or away? She did not know—she did not care. She simply leaped and ran— ran until she found herself alone amid the dead and the tall ramparts of towering buildings.

She stopped. She was alone. Alone! Alone on the streets —alone in the city—perhaps alone in the world! There crept in upon her the sense of deception—of creeping hands behind her back—of silent, moving things she could not see,—of voices hushed in fearsome conspiracy. She looked behind and sideways, started at strange sounds and heard still stranger, until every nerve within her stood sharp and quivering, stretched to scream at the barest touch. She whirled and flew back, whimpering like a child, until she found that narrow alley again and the dark, silent figure silhouetted at the top. She stopped and rested; then she walked silently toward him, looked at him timidly; but he said nothing as he handed her into the car. Her voice caught as she whispered:

"Not—that."

And he answered slowly: "No—not that!"

They climbed into the car. She bent forward on the

wheel and sobbed, with great, dry, quivering sobs, as they flew toward the cable office on the east side, leaving the world of wealth and prosperity for the world of poverty and work. In the world behind them were death and silence, grave and grim, almost cynical, but always decent; here it was hideous. It clothed itself in every ghastly form of terror, struggle, hate, and suffering. It lay wreathed in crime and squalor, greed and lust. Only in its dread and awful silence was it like to death everywhere.

Yet as the two, flying and alone, looked upon the horror of the world, slowly, gradually, the sense of all-enveloping death deserted them. They seemed to move in a world silent and asleep,—not dead. They moved in quiet reverence, lest somehow they wake these sleeping forms who had, at last, found peace. They moved in some solemn, world-wide *Friedhof*, above which some mighty arm had waved its magic wand. All nature slept until—until, and quick with the same startling thought, they looked into each other's eyes—he, ashen, and she, crimson, with unspoken thought. To both, the vision of a mighty beauty—of vast, unspoken things, swelled in their souls; but they put it away.

Great, dark coils of wire came up from the earth and down from the sun and entered this low lair of witchery. The gathered lightnings of the world centered here, binding with beams of light the ends of the earth. The doors gaped on the gloom within. He paused on the threshold.

"Do you know the code?" she asked.

"I know the call for help—we used it formerly at the bank."

She hardly heard. She heard the lapping of the waters far below,—the dark and restless waters—the cold and luring waters, as they called. He stepped within. Slowly she walked to the wall, where the water called below, and stood and waited. Long she waited, and he did not come. Then with a start she saw him, too, standing beside the black waters. Slowly he removed his coat and stood there silently. She walked quickly to him and laid her hand on his arm. He did not start or look. The waters lapped on in luring, deadly rhythm. He pointed down to the waters, and said quietly:

"The world lies beneath the waters now—may I go?"

She looked into his stricken, tired face, and a great pity surged within her heart. She answered in a voice clear and calm, "No."

Upward they turned toward life again, and he seized the wheel. The world was darkening to twilight, and a great, gray pall was falling mercifully and gently on the sleeping dead. The ghastly glare of reality seemed replaced with the dream of some vast romance. The girl lay silently back, as the motor whizzed along, and looked half-consciously for the elf-queen to wave life into this dead world again. She forgot to wonder at the quickness with which he had learned to drive her car. It seemed natural. And then as they whirled and swung into Madison Square and at the door of the Metropolitan Tower she gave a low cry, and her eyes were great! Perhaps she had seen the elf-queen?

The man led her to the elevator of the tower and deftly they ascended. In her father's office they gathered rugs and chairs, and he wrote a note and laid it on the desk; then they ascended to the roof and he made her comfortable. For a while she rested and sank to dreamy somnolence, watching the worlds above and wondering. Below lay the dark shadows of the city and afar was the shining of the sea. She glanced at him timidly as he set food before her and took a shawl and wound her in it, touching her reverently, yet tenderly. She looked up at him with thankfulness in her eyes, eating what he served. He watched the city. She watched him. He seemed very human,—very near now.

"Have you had to work hard?" she asked softly.

"Always," he said.

"I have always been idle," she said. "I was rich."

"I was poor," he almost echoed.

"The rich and the poor are met together," she began, and he finished:

"The Lord is the Maker of them all."

"Yes," she said slowly; "and how foolish our human distinctions seem—now," looking down to the great dead city stretched below, swimming in unlightened shadows.

"Yes—I was not—human, yesterday," he said.

She looked at him. "And your people were not my people," she said; "but today——" She paused. He was a man,—no more; but he was in some larger sense a gentleman,—sensitive, kindly, chivalrous, everything save his hands and—his face. Yet yesterday—

"Death, the leveler!" he muttered.

"And the revealer," she whispered gently, rising to her feet with great eyes. He turned away, and after fumbling a moment sent a rocket into the darkening air. It arose, shrieked, and flew up, a slim path of light, and, scattering its stars abroad, dropped on the city below. She scarcely noticed it. A vision of the world had risen before her. Slowly the mighty prophecy of her destiny overwhelmed her. Above the dead past hovered the Angel of Annunciation. She was no mere woman. She was neither high nor low, white nor black, rich nor poor. She was primal woman; mighty mother of all men to come and Bride of Life. She looked upon the man beside her and forgot all else but his manhood, his strong, vigorous manhood—his sorrow and sacrifice. She saw him glorified. He was no longer a thing apart, a creature below, a strange outcast of another clime and blood, but her Brother Humanity incarnate, Son of God and great All-Father of the race to be.

He did not glimpse the glory in her eyes, but stood looking outward toward the sea and sending rocket after rocket into the unanswering darkness. Dark-purple clouds lay banked and billowed in the west. Behind them and all around, the heavens glowed in dim, weird radiance that suffused the darkening world and made almost a minor music. Suddenly, as though gathered back in some vast hand, the great cloud-curtain fell away. Low on the horizon lay a long, white star—mystic, wonderful! And from it fled upward to the pole, like some wan bridal veil, a pale, wide sheet of flame that lighted all the world and dimmed the stars.

In fascinated silence the man gazed at the heavens and dropped his rockets to the floor. Memories of memories stirred to life in the dead recesses of his mind. The shackles seemed to rattle and fall from his soul. Up from the crass and crushing and cringing of his caste leaped the lone majesty of kings long dead. He arose within the shadows, tall, straight, and stern, with power in his eyes and ghostly scepters hovering to his grasp. It was as though some mighty Pharaoh lived again, or curled Assyrian lord. He turned and looked upon the lady, and found her gazing straight at him.

Silently, immovably, they saw each other face to face—eye to eye. Their souls lay naked to the night. It was not lust; it was not love—it was some vaster, mightier thing that needed neither touch of body nor thrill of soul. It was a thought divine, splendid.

Slowly, noiselessly, they moved toward each other—the heavens above, the seas around, the city grim and dead below. He loomed from out the velvet shadows vast and dark. Pearl-white and slender, she shone beneath the stars.

She stretched her jeweled hands abroad. He lifted up his mighty arms, and they cried each to the other, almost with one voice, "The world is dead."

"Long live the——"

"Honk! Honk!" Hoarse and sharp the cry of a motor drifted clearly up from the silence below. They started backward with a cry and gazed upon each other with eyes that faltered and fell, with blood that boiled.

"Honk! Honk! Honk! Honk!" came the mad cry again, and almost from their feet a rocket blazed into the air and scattered its stars upon them. She covered her eyes with her hands, and her shoulders heaved. He dropped and bowed, groped blindly on his knees about the floor. A blue flame spluttered lazily after an age, and she heard the scream of an answering rocket as it flew.

Then they stood still as death, looking to opposite ends of the earth.

"Clang—crash—clang!"

The roar and ring of swift elevators shooting upward from below made the great tower tremble. A murmur and babel of voices swept in upon the night. All over the once dead city the lights blinked, flickered, and flamed; and then with a sudden clanging of doors the entrance to the platform was filled with men, and one with white and flying hair rushed to the girl and lifted her to his breast. "My daughter!" he sobbed.

Behind him hurried a younger, comelier man, carefully clad in motor costume, who bent above the girl with passionate solicitude and gazed into her staring eyes until they narrowed and dropped and her face flushed deeper and deeper crimson.

"Julia," he whispered; "my darling, I thought you were gone forever."

She looked up at him with strange, searching eyes.

"Fred," she murmured, almost vaguely, "is the world—gone?"

"Only New York," he answered; "it is terrible—awful! You know,—but you, how did you escape—how have you endured this horror? Are you well? Unharmed?"

"Unharmed!" she said.

"And this man here?" he asked, encircling her drooping form with one arm and turning toward the Negro. Suddenly he stiffened and his hand flew to his hip. "Why!" he snarled. "It's—a—nigger—Julia! Has he—has he dared——"

She lifted her head and looked at her late companion curiously and then dropped her eyes with a sigh.

"He has dared—all, to rescue me," she said quietly, "and I—thank him—much." But she did not look at him again. As the couple turned away, the father drew a roll of bills from his pockets.

"Here, my good fellow," he said, thrusting the money into the man's hands, "take that,—what's your name?"

"Jim Davis," came the answer, hollow-voiced.

"Well, Jim, I thank you. I've always liked your people. If you ever want a job, call on me." And they were gone.

The crowd poured up and out of the elevators, talking and whispering.

"Who was it?"

"Are they alive?"

"How many?"

"Two!"

"Who was saved?"

"A white girl and a nigger—there she goes."

"A nigger? Where is he? Let's lynch the damned——"

"Shut up—he's all right—he saved her."

"Saved hell! He had no business——"

"Here he comes."

Into the glare of the electric lights the colored man moved slowly, with the eyes of those that walk and sleep.

"Well, what do you think of that?" cried a bystander; "of all New York, just a white girl and a nigger!"

The colored man heard nothing. He stood silently beneath the glare of the light, gazing at the money in his hand and shrinking as he gazed; slowly he put his other hand into his pocket and brought out a baby's filmy cap, and gazed again. A woman mounted to the platform and looked about, shading her eyes. She was brown, small, and toil-worn, and in one arm lay the corpse of a dark baby. The crowd parted and her eyes fell on the colored man; with a cry she tottered toward him.

"Jim!"

He whirled and, with a sob of joy, caught her in his arms.

A Hymn to the Peoples

O Truce of God!
And primal meeting of the Sons of Man,
Foreshadowing the union of the World!
From all the ends of earth we come!
Old Night, the elder sister of the Day,
Mother of Dawn in the golden East,
Meets in the misty twilight with her brood,
Pale and black, tawny, red and brown,
The mighty human rainbow of the world,
Spanning its wilderness of storm.

Softly in sympathy the sunlight falls,
Rare is the radiance of the moon;
And on the darkest midnight blaze the stars—
The far-flown shadows of whose brilliance
Drop like a dream on the dim shores of Time,
Forecasting Days that are to these
As day to night.

So sit we all as one.
So, gloomed in tall and stone-swathed groves,
The Buddha walks with Christ!
And Al-Koran and Bible both be holy!

Almighty Word!
In this Thine awful sanctuary,
First and flame-haunted City of the Widened World,
Assoil us, Lord of Lands and Seas!

We are but weak and wayward men,
Distraught alike with hatred and vainglory;
Prone to despise the Soul that breathes within—
High visioned hordes that lie and steal and kill,
Sinning the sin each separate heart disclaims,
Clambering upon our riven, writhing selves,
Besieging Heaven by trampling men to Hell!

We be blood-guilty! Lo, our hands be red!
Not one may blame the other in this sin!
But here—here in the white Silence of the Dawn,
Before the Womb of Time,
With bowéd hearts all flame and shame,
We face the birth-pangs of a world:
We hear the stifled cry of Nations all but born—
The wail of women ravished of their stunted brood!
We see the nakedness of Toil, the poverty of Wealth,
We know the Anarchy of Empire, and doleful Death of Life!
And hearing, seeing, knowing all, we cry:

Save us, World-Spirit, from our lesser selves!
Grant us that war and hatred cease,
Reveal our souls in every race and hue!
Help us, O Human God, in this Thy Truce,
To make Humanity divine!

CLASSICS *in* BLACK STUDIES SERIES

Anna E. Dickinson, *What Answer?*

Frederick Douglass, *My Bondage and My Freedom*

W. E. B. Du Bois, *Darkwater*

W. E. B. Du Bois, *The Negro*

Ida B. Wells-Barnett, *On Lynchings*